Regional Economic Diversification

Michael E. Conroy

The Praeger Special Studies program—utilizing the most modern and efficient book production techniques and a selective worldwide distribution network—makes available to the academic, government, and business communities significant, timely research in U.S. and international economic, social, and political development.

Regional Economic Diversification

PRAEGER SPECIAL STUDIES IN U.S. ECONOMIC, SOCIAL, AND POLITICAL ISSUES

Praeger Publishers   New York   Washington   London

Library of Congress Cataloging in Publication Data

Conroy, Michael E
    Regional Economic Diversification

    (Praeger special studies in U. S. economic,
social, and political issues)
    Bibliography: p.
    Includes index.
    1. Diversification of industry—United States.
2. Industries, Location of—United States.   I.   Title
HC110. D6C6   338'0973   74-9407
ISBN 0-275-05180-3

PRAEGER PUBLISHERS
111 Fourth Avenue, New York, N.Y. 10003, U.S.A.

Published in the United States of America in 1975
by Praeger Publishers, Inc.

Printed in the United States of America

ACKNOWLEDGMENTS

The roster of those to whom one is indebted by the time one has survived many years of formal education is invariably lengthy and can never be complete. The full sequence of events, influences, personalities, and impressions that determine such periods fade into obscurity not far behind the two or three most proximate links in the web of determination. I am indebted first and foremost to my parents, John T. Conroy, Sr. and Helen Z. Conroy, for the moral, intellectual, and financial support they extended with patience and persistence over many years of peripatetic studies. To them this book is dedicated.

Among those directly influential in the formulation of this study, I am especially grateful to the following: Frank L. Keller at Tulane University introduced me to the topic of industrial location subsidies; Hugh O. Nourse, now at the University of Missouri at St. Louis, taught me that regional economics can be both theoretically stimulating and empirically and operationally satisfying; Harold F. Williamson, Jr., as supervisor of the thesis that grew into this book, exercised an appreciated combination of stimulus and control; and my fellow graduate students at the University of Illinois, who were ever willing to listen to another formulation of the problem, lightened through their camaraderie the burden of the least pleasant periods of research.

I am also grateful for the assistance I have received on this project in the past two years from my colleagues at the University of Texas, especially Allan King, David Kendrick, Charles Knapp, and Alfred Norman. Without the cheerful, competent, and meticulous editorial advice of Sandra Hooper and Charlotte Smith, who typed the many drafts, the present version of the study would be far less coherent, consistent, and aesthetically pleasing. Finally, I wish to acknowledge the enormous amount of support of many sorts that I have received over the past four years of work on this study from my wife, Judy, and from our children.

The first three chapters constitute the majority of my Ph.D. dissertation [8] written at the University of Illinois at Urbana-Champaign and reproduced here with the permission of the Board of Regents of that institution. Small portions of Chapters 1 and 3 have appeared in a recent article in the Southern Economic Journal [6]; some of Chapter 2 has appeared in Regional and Urban Economics [7]; and a much-reduced version of Chapter 5 was published in the Journal of Regional Science [5]. All such material is reproduced with the authorization of the editors of the respective journals.

CONTENTS

LIST OF TABLES

TABLES IN THE APPENDIXES

LIST OF FIGURES

At any moment there exists a finite total world demand for economic activity and thus a finite quantity of income generated by it. Over any given period of time there will occur a finite change in the demand for economic activity. The spatial or geographic distribution of that limited economic activity and, hence, the spatial distribution of the income generated is the product of a set of processes that are inherently competitive. Though it may be possible to specify a pareto-optimal spatial equilibrium distribution of economic activity for the globe as a whole such that world income is maximized, the distribution of that income among the various spatial subdivisions or among their political counterparts remains a source of intense competition. If all factors of production were perfectly mobile across relevant space or if the opportunity costs of transporting goods were zero and all goods were perfectly mobile, then spatial competition would disappear. In fact, however, the fundamental economic objectives of nations, states, cities, and smaller spatially delimited organizations, ranging from increased real income per capita to improved stability and interpersonal income distribution, are related to the spatial competition for economic activity in a manner and to a degree often overlooked.

This spatial competition is not an artifact of competitive "market" economies, but rather arises strictly from the fact that the global economy has been fragmented into multiple semiautonomous economies, each of which seeks to maximize the return to its "own" factors of production. Even in the centralized economies where the least mobile factors—land, mineral resources, and productive capital—are owned and managed by the society as a whole and where as a consequence intranational spatial competition may have been reduced substantially, the international competition for the location of economic activity is of critical importance to the extent that relative levels of income among nations are of concern.

For years now, development planning bodies on almost every conceivable level have adopted policies that have attempted to reap the benefits of additional economic activity by stimulating the location of new, expanded, or relocated activities within specific areal confines. The policy measures that have been and continue to be used within the United States to pursue this goal—ranging from the simple provision of information on the locational characteristics of an area to outright construction and leasing of new manufacturing plants—represent public intervention on a massive scale in the spatial allocation of economic activity. These policies typically consist of either implicit or explicit public investment in that activity. To the extent that the policies are successful in inducing the increased local economic activity, they become public investment in the specific activities attracted.

Tax exemptions to newly locating or expanding firms are one of the clearest forms in which the process is seen, for they tend to represent additional tax burdens accepted by the populace of a region in expectation of derived benefits. Public investment in vocational education, focused mass transit, and even expenditures on local public recreational facilities (which raise nonpecuniary local income) can be interpreted, in part, as a subsidy of this sort. Financial assistance to the organizers of economic activities and public investment in some economic infrastructure, such as roads, railheads, waterways, and industrial parks, are further common examples. On an international level, restriction of trade through quotas, tariffs, and restrictive agreements in order to stimulate economic activity within the "protected" geographic area also represents an implicit process of public investment in the specific favored activities.

The magnitude of such interventions in the spatial allocation of economic activity within the United States is somewhat surprising in view of the presumption of independent competitive spatial allocation generally found in the theoretical literature. As of 1971 there were no fewer than 4,513 different organizations actively involved in "industrial development," the vast majority of them seeking to attract new or expanded industry to specific, very limited geographic areas [22, pp. 195-226]. The tools at their disposal are formidable.

No fewer than 42 of the 50 states provide legal bases for city and/or county revenue bond financing of new industries, and 26 states provide for state financing for expansion of existing plants [22, p. 185]. In 13 states such financing may, by law, extend to 100 percent of the cost of a new facility at interest rates ranging from below the prime rate to no more than 10 percent. The total amount shown by one survey to have been spent on such state and local financing of completely private plants by 27 states exceeded $4.9 billion in 1971 [22, p. 184].

For 16 of those states for which comparable data were available, the breakdown for 1968 and 1971 and the rate of growth of public industrial development financing is given in Table I.1. The 16 states included there accounted for 87.8 percent of the 27-state 1971 total given above.

In 42 states there exist city- and/or county-owned industrial park sites; in 12 states, cities and counties provide free land. In 21 states corporate income tax exemption is available to new industries; in 20 states personal income tax is waived for varying periods. In addition, some states provide sales-tax exemption on raw material inputs (39), plant-specific vocational training (49), state-supported research on local and potentially local state-export products (42), and tax exemptions or moratoria on land and capital improvements (17) and on equipment or machinery (21) [22, pp. 186-87].

The relevance of viewing such policy measures as investment in specific activities or industries arises from the fact that nowhere in the literature does there exist either a consideration of the relative rates of return on the public investment to the "public" that is investing in such

expansion industries or a procedure for maximizing that return in terms
of choosing either expansion industries or appropriate levels of subsidy.
It is to that general problem that this study is directed.

TABLE I. 1

Industrial Development Bond Financing
by 16 States and Their Political Subdivisions
(in millions of dollars, cumulative to date)

State	1968	1971	Percent Increase (1968-71)
Alabama	748. 5	860. 0	14. 8
Arkansas	496. 1	621. 1	25. 1
Georgia	225. 0	258. 5	14. 8
Kansas	104. 8	180. 2	71. 9
Kentucky	395. 7	640. 9	61. 9
Louisiana	231. 4	346. 2	49. 6
Maine	3. 3	6. 3	90. 9
Maryland	18. 6	21. 0	12. 9
Missouri	103. 2	238. 7	131. 2
Nebraska	81. 4	115. 8	42. 2
Ohio	145. 0	365. 0	151. 7
Oklahoma	63. 5	334. 0	525. 9
South Carolina	50. 0	180. 0	360. 0
Virginia	8. 3	115. 0	1285. 5
West Virginia	45. 0	51. 0	44. 1
Wyoming	20. 0	55. 0	175. 0
Total	2, 739. 9	4, 388. 7	60. 1

Source: Industrial Development Research Institute. Site Selection
Handbook, 1971. Vol. 2. Atlanta: Conway Research Corporation, 1971.

THE CENTRAL FOCUS

The set of motives that may lead planners and promoters to attempt
to attract increased economic activity to a region is of considerable size.
The desire for simple increases in the aggregate level of income or of
income per capita in the region offers one such motive. Pursuit of
increases in returns to immobile factors is another. A third motive is
an interest in stabilizing (in the sense of reducing fluctuations over time)

the levels of aggregate income, employment, or other regional economic characteristics. The reduction of such "instability" poses a particularly interesting problem because it involves, inherently, a factor of uncertainty about such economic "returns" from any given economic structure and a factor interdependence among components of that structure.

Fluctuations in selected characteristics of regional economies have been the subject of analytical efforts for nearly as long as regional economics has been a recognized subdiscipline within economics. The intuitive policy solution, creating or acquiring some form of "diversity" or "diversification" in industrial structure, has also been a venerable component of the literature. In Chapter 1 of this study, the history of such analysis is surveyed and some of the major conceptual and empirical problems heretofore hindering the analysis of industrial diversification are noted.

The central focus for this study consists of an analysis of the industrial structure of regions under conditions of uncertainty about the returns that such structures will bring to the region. The risk of fluctuations of varying magnitude is juxtaposed with the returns from alternative structures. In Chapter 2 a model is developed that is used to demonstrate that in most cases a "diversified" industrial structure will be the most efficient form for trading-off the risks and returns of alternative industrial structures. The nature of this "diversification" is specified precisely and a theoretical measure of relative diversification is derived.

This measure of diversification is then used in Chapter 3 to test whether those regions, among a sample of 52 U.S. Standard Metropolitan Statistical Areas (SMSAs), that possessed the greatest theoretical diversification experienced the greatest stability in manufacturing employment over a recent ten-year period. The trade-off between growth rates and stability and growth rates and diversification are also explored. Additionally, a number of further hypotheses with respect to industrial diversification and a set of alternative measures of diversity are discussed.

This attempt at defining more clearly the concept of industrial diversification and of specifying more precisely how such may be measured is merely a first step, though a crucial one, toward the more important goal of determining what level of subsidy, if any, is justified in the pursuit of greater stability in regional economic activity. It is to be hoped that conceptual and empirical results of this study will make the latter goal more easily attainable.

To the extent that an "optimally diversified" industrial structure is potentially identifiable for a given region, it is of importance to know whether market location processes in a largely competitive economy are capable of leading to a structure that approximates the diversified target structure. A very preliminary exploration of market location processes under uncertainty with respect to regional wage levels is undertaken in Chapter 4. It is noted there that there is reason to believe that there exists a class of diversification-related pecuniary external economies that make it unlikely that market location processes will permit a "diversifying" industry to reap the full benefits of its effects upon the regional economy or force a "destabilizing" industry to internalize the full negative impact it may have on regional competitiveness. The need for an extramarket location subsidy-tax scheme for the sake of diversifying local economic activity thus appears legitimate.

Given a desire to diversify local economic activity and a willingness to appropriate funds for diversification subsidies, there remain several fundamentally empirical questions of importance to planners and policy makers: (1) Can optimally diversifying changes in industrial structure be identified for specific preexisting industrial structures? (2) Are there merely a small number of nationally stable industries for which all diversifying regional economies will be competing? or (3) Will nationally stable industries be the optimally diversifying additions to widely differing local economies? Chapter 5 presents three alternative approaches to the problem of defining diversification strategies and a comparison of both their potential effect and the composititon of the changes in structure as suggested by each. The results of simulated changes in the structure of economic activity reported there provide preliminary evidence that significant changes in some characteristics of instability can be achieved, that nationally stable industries are seldom optimally diversifying, and that, therefore, widespread diversification efforts do not necessarily imply fruitless competition for a few stabilizing industries.

The conceptual treatment and rudimentary empirical analysis presented in this volume represent, at best, an attempt to return the notion of local influence over the stability of local economic activity to the realm of respectable regional economic research. It appears that frustration over the gulf between the conceptualization of regional diversity or diversification and the trend of mainstream analytical economics has lessened the interest shown by regional economists in the potential of local diversification efforts. If, on the other hand, greater credence is lent to the potential efficacy of local efforts and increased local effort results, there will arise additional need for analysis of the national significance of increased competitiveness in the influences determining patterns of location for economic activity. Reduced local fluctuations may lead to increased stability in the national economy, as suggested in Chapter 2. Whether the cumulative costs of such diversification will generate increases in national competitiveness or whether, on the contrary, they will lead to inefficient reallocation of resources to expanding or newly established plants in excess of the value of their stabilizing influence awaits further research of now-greater importance.

Regional Economic Diversification

1

THE CONCEPT OF DIVERSIFICATION IN THE CONTEXT OF STRUCTURAL ANALYSIS OF REGIONAL FLUCTUATIONS

The study of diversification of regional industrial structure in order to reduce the severity of regional fluctuations in economic activity is a logical outgrowth of the extensive analysis of the origins and nature of such fluctuations and of appropriate policies to counteract them. Regional fluctuations in employment, income, or the general level of economic activity have been the subject of theoretical analysis and some empirical testing since the very earliest recognition that subnational regions possessed definable economies meriting separate attention. Regional stabilization policy to counteract such fluctuations has been approached from several distinct vantage points and for at least two relatively distinct purposes. On the one hand, during the late 1940s and early 1950s the relationship between regional fluctuations and national fluctuations, where the implied causation ran from the regional level to the national level, was studied as a part of the analysis of national business cycles prevalent then. The works of Vining [75], Kidner [24], and Simpson [54] fall in this category. On the other hand, the vein of inquiry that has persisted much more visibly in the literature is that which examines the relationship between economic structure of different regions and their relative responsiveness to national fluctuations in economic activity. The further works of Vining [73, 74, 76] as well as those of Thompson [57, 58], Hanna [19], Neff [36], Neff and Weifenbach [37], Williams [77], Garbarino [14], Borts [3], Siegel [53], and Cutler and Hansz [10] are representative of this interest.

The existence of this latter body of literature and the persistence with which additions are made to it are both reflections of the strong intuitive appeal of the central concept that underlies it. In the words of Wilbur Thompson [57, p. 16]:

Nothing could seem more certain, deductively, than a close, causal relationship between the local industry mix and the cyclical instability of that area. Local business cycles would seem to reflect in large part the cyclical characteristics of its principal exports. . . .

1

The conclusion offered by empirical research in the area to date, however, has been less than satisfying. Isard suggested in 1960 that the available information presented a "clouded picture," one in which it could only be said that "the cyclical responsiveness of any given region cannot be divorced entirely from its industrial composition. . . ." [23, pp. 187-88]. More recently, Richardson concluded in his survey of the area that "the overwhelming consensus of evidence is that the residual (to be explained after the effects of industrial composition have been exhausted) is large, and regional cycles cannot be primarily explained by industrial composition" [43, p. 277].

Such pessimism may be premature. The theoretical models that underlie many of the most important empirical studies (those most often cited) suffer from several major conceptual and practical problems. In the first place, most of the studies undertaken to date have been restricted to very high levels of aggregation both in the size of the area dealt with (for example, whole states by Borts [3]) and in the level of industrial categories. Second, this latter problem reflects an even greater difficulty inherent in defining "industrial composition" excessively narrowly. For example, Siegel [53] and Cutler and Hansz [10] used "the percent of employment in durable goods manufacturing" in the two most recent studies. Third, the quantity and quality of data brought to bear upon the empirical testing of the hypothesis, as well as the quantitative techniques used in all but the most recent analyses, require that the "overwhelming consensus" noted by Richardson be treated with some circumspection.

One subset of this literature, that pertaining to the "diversity" or "diversification" of regional economic activity and its relationship to relative regional fluctuations, has encountered similar conceptual and practical difficulties and has engendered similar pessimism. Conceptually, the potential of diversification efforts (never clearly and precisely defined) has been minimized by the approach found in Thompson (and echoed in Richardson [43, p. 276] and elsewhere), which suggests that "all urban areas cannot possess the relatively few stable industries" and that "industrial diversification leads toward a cycle pattern approximating that of the national economy. . ." [57, p. 148].

In fact, as will be demonstrated in Chapters 2 and 3, diversification on the basis of reducing expected fluctuations in aggregate regional economic activity can lead to regional stability considerably greater than that of the nation as a whole. To the extent that such proves to be possible, reduction in average regional fluctuations will stabilize the national economy. For national fluctuations have no life of their own; they are nothing more than weighted averages of regional fluctuations [74, p. 186].

A further difficulty encountered in evaluating diversification strategies has been the lack of a conceptual framework for defining and measuring "diversification." Is it sufficient to increase the number of "different" industries? In what way should industries be "different"? Does this not run counter to the advantages of "specialization"? The imprecision with which these questions have been dealt has, we suspect, increased the difficulty of measuring diversification in industrial structures and of assessing the value of diversification as a policy objective.

The critical review that follows of a sample of the most prominent studies in structural analysis of regional fluctuations and in diversification of regional structures is designed with two objectives in mind: (1) to dispel some of the pessimism with respect to studies of regional industrial structure, and (2) to develop a context within which the subsequent reformulation of the problem may be viewed.

STUDIES OF REGIONAL FLUCTUATIONS AND INDUSTRIAL STRUCTURE

The concept that economies characterized by specialization in the production of durable goods would experience greater fluctuations than those encountered in economies less specialized in this direction is traceable at least to J. M. Clark in the early 1930s [4, p. 75]. It is of particular interest to note that Clark may be considered a direct precursor of the theoretical analysis to follow in this study. He viewed aggregate fluctuations in economic activity as a function of the proportions of productive resources given over to the production of different classes of goods. The relevant "difference" in his analysis was the relative responsiveness of production of a good to national levels of economic activity.

Vining, Neff and Weifenbach, Williams, Garbarino, and Hanna

In 1945, 1946, and 1949, Vining published three pioneering theoretical discussions of the potential relevance of a "regional" analysis of the U.S. economy for purposes of analyzing business cycles [74, 75, 76]. He theorized that if regional exports could be distinguished from regional imports along relatively broad lines, the region that would suffer most, in a given national decline in income, would be that region that exported products with high-income elasticities of demand and that imported products with low-income elasticities of demand. The presumed regional balance-of-payments problem was expected to lead to reductions in local bank reserves and, consequently, to multiplied local contraction.

In his empirical analyses he demonstrated the appropriateness of viewing national cycles as a weighted function of state cycles [74]; he noted that the industrial composition and relative cycles of state income tended to substantiate his income-elasticity hypothesis [73], and he found two cities that also substantiated the hypothesis at the level of more-meaningful "economic regions" [75].

3

There also appeared in 1949 two studies designed to examine the issue more definitively. Neff and Weifenbach [36, 37] explored the differences in the timing, duration, and amplitude of cycles in six major industrial urban areas from 1919 to 1945. Their analysis was based upon visual interpretation of time-series bar graphs for each city. On each such graph the turning points for major economic series in each area had been superimposed, and the relative pattern of onset and duration of cycles was compared with a priori knowledge of very general industrial characteristics. They found little or no relationship between rates of growth of employment and income in the regions and the timing or duration of regional cycles, some relationship between "industrial pattern" and timing and duration (although "not in any simple and direct manner"), and a relationship between "divergent economic pattern" (strong specialization) and amplitude of fluctuation only where "the divergence is extreme" [36, pp. 115-19]. Given the imprecision of the empirical technique, this last inference might be interpreted to suggest not that the relationship exists only when the divergence is extreme, but rather that it appeared only when such was the case.

In 1950 Williams [77] improved upon the empirical technique of Neff and Weifenbach. He tested the significance of specialization in the manufacturing sector of 13 U.S. cities based on the percentage of manufacturing wage earners in nondurable manufacturing industries. He used an index of stability for each city composed of the ration of central city retail sales in 1933 to the average of such sales in 1929 and 1937. He found a rank correlation of .84 between the two measures (significant at less than .01) and concluded that industrial compostion and the amplitude of cyclical fluctuation were, in fact, correlated "to some degree" [77, p. 50].

The major weaknesses of Williams' study are the two indices that he uses. Use of employment in all nondurable manufacturing as a percentage of total manufacturing employment as a measure of the nature of the industrial composition requires strong assumptions. It must be assumed, for example, that employment in all industries within non-durables have identical distributions of employment over time. That is, all pair-wise correlation coefficients among nondurable goods industries are assumed to be 1.0. It must also be assumed that all industries in durable goods have distributions that are independent of nondurable goods production (correlation coefficients of 0.0). Though such assumptions might be tenable at the 5- or 6-digit Standard Industrial Classification (SIC) level and might be made with difficulty at the 3- or 4-digit level, they are heroic at this level, essentially 1-digit SIC.

Williams utilized an index of instability for each city, which consisted of the ratio of the dollar volume of retail sales in 1933 (presumed cycle trough) to the average of 1929 and 1937 sales. This measure can be questioned on two counts. First, the measure will rank any two cities in appropriate order only if both had retail sales that decreased monotonically from 1929 to 1933 and increased monotonically from

4

1933 to 1937. Second, instability in retail sales is not necessarily causally related to the percentage of manufacuring employment in nondurables, unless manufacturing employment is a very large proportion of total urban employment. For comparisons across cities, the relationship between retail sales and nondurable manufacturing may be assumed identical only if manufacturing is assumed or is demonstrated to comprise a constant proportion of the labor force. Nonetheless, Williams' study represented a significant improvement in the quantification of the interrelationship between industrial composition and some measure of relative stability.

Two studies reported in 1954 shed additional light on the problem. Garbarino [14] analyzed the distribution of unemployment in 1950 among the nine major census regions and across a selected sample of manufacturing industries. He found that the standard deviation in percentage unemployment rates within the industries across the nine regions was slightly greater (1.47) than the variation in unemployment rates across industries within regions (1.13). Given the enormity of the regions encompassed and the very small sample of industries included, Garbarino felt required to qualify his results substantially [14, p. 32]:

> While this limited exploration does not permit general conclusions as to the relationship between regional and industrial differences in unemployment, it does suggest that regional differences may well be something more than another dimension of industrial differences and worthy of analysis in their own right.

In that same year, Hanna [19] provided a "new attempt to separate and measure [the] combination of cyclical, secular, and random elements" that determine state per capita income. Using a "sensitivity index" consisting of the elasticity of state income with respect to national income, he found that states with a high proportion of employment in agriculture tended to be more sensitive to changes in national income than those with high proportions in durable and nondurable goods manufacture [19, p. 328]. This result concurred with observations by Vining [73].

Vining theorized in this regard that, although one generally considers that food products and similar agricultural goods have low-income elasticities of demand, in fact the raw material nature of many agricultural products as inputs into industrial processes actually gives them relatively high-income elasticities of demand, at least in the short run. The nature of the demand for cotton and soybeans are examples of this.

The single most detailed and comprehensive study to date in the area is that of Borts [3]. Concentrating on manufacturing employment in 33 states, he used National Bureau of Economic Research (NBER)-defined peaks and troughs for three periods of business contraction and expansion—1919-1921-1923, 1929-1933-1937, and 1948-1949-1953—to study the relationship between relative state contraction and expansion and the respective industrial compositions.

For each state he calculated "the cycle the nation would have if each national industry were given the weight it has in a particular state." He then compared those cycles based on individual state industrial composition with those known for the nation. He concluded that "the most variable states are characterized by a high proportion of durable-goods manufacture, specifically transportation equipment, . . . primary and fabricated metal products, machinery and lumber. The least variable states are characterized by nondurable manufactures: textiles, shoes, apparel, tobacco and food products" [3, pp. 157-58].

While Borts' approach was ingenious in the context of those that had preceded it, it suffered from one critical flaw. In order to use the simple unweighted proportions of 2-digit SIC manufacturing employment in each state as his industrial composition variable, he was led to assume that "each state industry behaves in the same fashion as its national counterpart, so that the only difference among states is the relative importance accorded to these national cyclical impluses" [3, p. 170]. Such an assumption would be true only if either (1) all production in every state is solely for final consumption (that is, no intermediate production), or (2) the interindustry linkages were identical for every industry in every state. This latter assumption is by far the more harsh of the two, for it suggests not only that interindustry coefficients are identical but also that the proportions of gross output going to each intermediate demanding industry and to final demand for each plant of an industry must be identical across the nation.

But an industry in a region could deviate from its national pattern simply because the set of industries it is supplying in its region is different from the national set. And such a deviation is attributable to the industrial composition of the region. More specifically, a fall in final demand, nationally, for a given final good such as automobiles, might reduce demand for finished autos by an equal percentage at each of 10 spatially differentiated assembly plants. But it would have a particularly multiplied impact upon a regional economy that contained many suppliers of automobile components even though the percentage of the labor force employed in auto assembly (or the percentage of regional value-added derived from it) was the same as that of other regions.

Borts' study, then, will have underestimated the variability attributable to industrial composition. It may have captured the impact of all industries producing solely for local final demand (that is, consumption or export from the state); but it omitted the internal multiplication of such impacts in those regions where some portion of the intermediate products used were also produced locally.

Although Borts did not quantify the explanatory powers of the industrial compostition variable, it appears that his work is that which is most frequently in mind when one reads of the limited value of the variable. His qualitative conclusions were strongly qualified, and these qualifications seem to carry over to some of the subsequent less-ambitious studies that have attempted quantification.

One such more recent study, that of Siegel [53], incorporated a considerably improved measure of instability but fell back upon the crudest measure of industrial composition. He used the coefficient of variation of the residuals around a linear regression of time on total manufacturing employment in each of 31 SMSAs over the period 1949-62 to obtain a trend- and size-corrected measure of fluctuations. He then calculated a rank correlation coefficient of .71 between the index and the percentage of total manufacturing employment engaged in durable goods manufacture. Squaring it to obtain a coefficient of determination of .50 he suggested that half of the variation in amplitude of total manufacturing employment between SMSAs is explained by the proportion of manufacturing employment in durable goods.

Given the imprecision and difficult implicit assumptions of Siegel's measure of industrial composition, one is led to suggest that refinement of the measure would be very likely to increase the explanatory power of the variable. For by identifying those industries that are in fact the least stable over time from among both durables and nondurables and by regrouping them into more meaningful combinations based upon such instability, the unexplained residual could be expected to decrease.

The most recent study of industrial structure and relative fluctuations was undertaken by Cutler and Hansz [10]. Using quarterly data on nonagricultural employment and bank debits in 35 SMSAs from 1961 through 1968, they constructed a sensitivity index for each that consisted of the ration of "acceleration" or "deceleration" in each to the average for all 35 metropolitan areas. "Acceleration" and "deceleration" were defined as the quarterly percentage changes in the basic series in selected quarters that showed "an unusually large increase within the 1961-68 period" or "an unusually small increase or decline" in the raw data.

They then calculated the simple correlation coefficients between this index and three measures of industrial composition. They found significant positive correlation in all three cases: employment in durable goods as a percentage of all manufacturing employment, .361; employment in durable goods as a percentage of total employment, .449; and manufacturing employment as a percentage of total employment, .337. They also found much higher levels of correlation between industrial composition and sensitivity to national fluctuations in the 16 Northeast-North Central SMSAs.

They concluded [10, p. 27]:

What can the public administrator who is planning the industrialization of his metropolitan area gain from the above findings? He may conclude from our findings that it is probably not a myth that the differences among industry composition will have differential effects on metropolitan performance. Previous literature on this subject might well have left a doubtful impression. Although not purporting to be a final resolution, our findings point definitely towards a connection between industrial composition and sensitivity to fluctuations.

The accuracy and appropriateness of their index of instability is difficult to evaluate since the precise criteria for determining the inputs into their ratios are not given. But the further substantiation of the basic hypothesis provided by this independent data and alternative technique, albeit of a highly aggregated form, may be viewed as encouraging.

STUDIES OF URBAN INDUSTRIAL DIVERSIFICATION

If the sensitivity of a region, say a metropolitan area, to fluctuations in the national economy is a function of its industrial composition to some significant extent, the next logical question that a policy maker would raise is, "What type of industrial structure is characteristic of the more stable regions?"

Several of the studies cited yielded an initial response to that question by the choice of durable goods manufacturing as an index of industrial composition. It is relatively clear, then, that specialization in durable goods manurfacuring will, ceteris paribus, lead to greater relative instability over time in the level of regional economic activity. Yet "durable goods" includes an enormous range of different industries, even where such "differences" are seen only as different SIC categories based on differences in production techniques.

A number of alternative measures of industrial diversity or diversification have been offered over the past 40 years. Very few of these have been tested against the actual experiences of different regions with respect to stability.

All of the measures of industrial diversification proposed to date share a pair of potentially crippling conceptual defects. First, there is generally a lack of precise specification of either the specific form of instability against which one is diversifying or the relevant set of "differences" among industries presumably incorporated in the measures. Second, most measures have presupposed that there must exist a norm for each industry in each region and that relative concentration or diversification must be measured with respect to such norm.

8

Measures of Industrial Diversity

Bahl et al. [2] have recently surveyed and compared a set of seven measures of industrial diversity. They note that they may be divided into three classes based on the nature of the "normal" proportion of employment assumed for each industry in each region.

One group of measures has implicitly used the U.S. national average employment or value-added in each industry as the basis of comparison. Florence [13], for example, calculated for each state an index based upon absolute deviations from the U.S. average in each industry. The study by Borts [3], discussed above, implicitly uses the U.S. percentage distribution of employment among industries as the norm. Steigenga [55] calculated the variance of the distribution of percentage employed across 25 classes. As noted by Bahl, this measure also uses national average employment in each industry as the norm with respect to which deviations (here squared) are measured.

An alternative approach has consisted of comparing actual distributions of employment to a hypothetical rectangular distribution representing "balanced" industrial composition (equal percentages in each group). McLaughlin [34] computed concentration ratios for 14 U.S. cities based on the percentage of total value-added in manufacture for each city derived from the five (and the ?1) leading manufacturing industries in each. Although he sought to measure the diversification of each city, where this was conceived to be associated with introducing "more types of production and trade" [34, p. 133], McLaughlin's measure was inappropriate first in that "balanced" composition would be represented by different percentages in each city since, as he noted, there were substantial differences in the number of industries tallied in each city. Thus, if a city k possessed n_k industries, the optimal diversification implied here would have to be $\frac{1}{n_k}$ of total value-added derived from each. But since n_k varied across cities, $\frac{1}{n_k}$ would vary for reasons other than relative concentration or diversification.

Tress [61] also constructed an index of diversity or diversification of this second type. He corrected for the first error in McLaughlin's index (although apparently unknowingly) by calculating deviations in each city from equal distribution across a specified set of 12 comprehensive industry classes (essentially 1-digit SIC), thus expecting $\frac{1}{n_k}$ = 8.3 percent for each industry in each city for perfectly "balanced" composition. Bahl et al. modified this measure by computing deviations from equal distribution among 39 industry classes (that is, 2.56 percent in each class).

This general approach is called the "ogive" technique because it is effectively identical to that of Rodgers [45], who constructed cumulative frequency distributions (ogives) for percentage employed across a given number of industries and then calculated a quasi-gini coefficient for the derived Lorenz distributions. The approaches are identical in that equal distribution among the industries measured would yield maximum "diversity," and deviations from such a distribution are given as indications of meaningful specialization.

Both the national average norm and the equal distribution norm suffer from an additional difficulty, slightly distinct from that noted for McLaughlin's version, in that they are inherently biased in favor of larger cities. Both measures give very heavy weight to the absence of a particular industry from a particular area. Given any specific number of industrial classifications, the smaller the city the more likely it is that one or more industry groups will not be represented. Bahl noted that even with his 39 industry classifications (more industries than those included in the reference group of any other study), the bias became evident in the empirical results.

The most empirically sophisticated class of measures suggested to date is the minimum requirements approach of Ullman and Dacey [63, 64]. For them, the "normal" employment in each SIC category in each city is given by the percentage that will theoretically just satisfy local needs. Such minimum-requirements norms are calculated on the basis of cross-section regression analysis of the minimum percentage in each industry employed in cities of different size classes. The norms thus calculated are not independent of the size classes chosen, and they reduce to use of the "national average" in the limiting case where the minimum is invariant with population size class.

The "minimum-requirements" approach highlights most clearly the further conceptual difficulty that permeates all three classes of measures of diversification, the very concept of a "normal" proportion of industry.

If the location of industries within a supraregional area is to be viewed as a process in which the optimal location for a plant producing a specific product is a function of the location and the geographic size of the market as well as the location of inputs and the transport costs of inputs and outputs, then a "normal" quantity of any given industry in any given area has relevance only where the areal extent of the market is very small. One would expect every region to have a "normal" quantity of a specific industry only if the market area for the product was no larger than the region. For comparisons within population size groups, the only appropriate industries would be those possessing market areas no larger than the smallest regions within each size group. This can be seen most clearly by noting that if an industry in one region could serve not only its own population but also some of that of any contiguous region (that is, market area greater than the size of the region in which the producer is located), then it would be unreasonable to expect that both regions would have identical quantities or any fixed quantity of that industry even if they were identical in population size.

It is further inappropriate to suggest that if an industry is present in a region that the size of that industry should, in general, bear some fixed relationship to the population, size, or income of the region. The size of the market area for a plant in any specific region is closely related to such measures of the size of the region only where market areas are smaller than or identical to the size of the region or where the region is closed to interregional trade.

Measurement of industrial diversification relative to a "norm" in terms of expected or "balanced" distributions of industry are thus appropriate for those industries that are essentially "nonbasic" or local-consumption oriented. But the industries with which one is most interested, the industries that can serve as a vehicle for interregional transmission of fluctuations, and the industries with respect to which a region can meaningfully "specialize" are the "basic" or predominantly export-oriented industries (necessarily industries with market areas larger than the region as a whole) that are the basis for analysis in terms of relative regional fluctuations.

Requisites of a Theoretically Ideal Measure
of Relative Diversification

Diversification, n. 1. the act or state of diversifying. . . .

Diversify, v. 1. to make diverse, as in form or character; give variety or diversity to. . . . 2. to invest in different types of (securities, investments, etc.) or produce different types of (manufactured products, crops, etc.). . . .[1]

The construction of an appropriate measure of industrial diversification for regions requires first that the appropriate "differences" or "diversity" in the form or character of industries be identified. Only then will it be possible to specify the further conditions required of a measure of such diversity. In the discussion that follows immediately, we shall attempt to define in general terms the appropriate set of differences among industries and the additional characteristics of an "ideal" index of diversification. The measure derived in Chapter 2, it will be shown there, is one member of what may be a set of such indices.

The first restriction on relevant differences among industries relates to the purpose for which diversification is undertaken. Diversification undertaken, for example, in order to reduce the significance of or eliminate some forms of pollution would evaluate relevant differences among industries in terms of the amount and nature of production by-products. Diversification as discussed here pertains to the reduction of fluctuations over time in the levels of regional economic aggregates such as income, employment, and other measures. The appropriate

---

1. The Random House Dictionary of the English Language (The Unabridged Edition) (New York: Random House, 1968), p. 388.

differences among industries are thus those that contribute to different patterns of aggregate fluctuations when they are combined.

The traditional basis for difference among industries has been the set of groupings that has evolved over time as the Standard Industrial Classification code. It has generally been assumed that merely because one industry is classified in one SIC group and another is classified in another group, those two industries are more "different" from one another in a relevant way than they are from other members of their classification group. On this basis, it is generally reasoned, diversification in terms of investing in numerically different SIC products is diversification in a sense relevant to the objective. Two dissenting arguments need to be made.

First, the SIC classification scheme was never intended for such purposes. Industries are classified in the code according to very general considerations of inputs, outputs, and processes of production. The Office of Statistical Standards states formally only that [69, p. 612]:

> an industry is a grouping of establishments primarily engaged in the same or similar lines of economic activity. In the manufacturing division, the line of activity is generally defined in terms of the product made, materials consumed, or process of manufacture used.

If the differences between two establishments that are relevant to a specific form of diversification are precisely captured by the overall differences between the two SIC groups to which they are assigned, then the resulting SIC classification will be all that is needed to distinguish among them. But the probability of such a concurrence of criteria is very small.

Second, use of SIC differences alone implies that the magnitude of differences between any two pairs of SIC groups is identical. That is, any two SIC groups are just as "different" from one another as they are from any third group. It is intuitively clear, however, that some SIC codes are very much "more different" from any given code than are others. It is not sufficient to assume that presence in a numerically different SIC class, at any level of disaggregation, reflects the "differences" relevant to diversification for the purpose of reducing regional fluctuations. Thus, the simple addition of SIC-different industries to an industry mix will not necessarily diversify it in the appropriate sense, or, most certainly, not in an efficient form, that is, at least cost.

If each industry in a region is assumed to exist and to contribute to aggregate fluctuations in economic activity independently, then the appropriate differences among such industries are their independent tendencies to fluctuate over time in response to fluctuations in intermediate and final demand for their respective products. It is on this basis, for example, that "durable goods industries" have generally been juxtaposed with "nondurables." It has been observed for many years that those SIC groups included in durable goods tend as a group to fluctuate considerably more over time, particularly in the medium term and especially in terms of their "responsiveness" to "national cycles." But not all industries within durable goods will fluctuate more than any industry in nondurables, and much further disaggregation is necessary.

If each industry in a region is viewed, more realistically, as having definite interrelationships with the other industries in the region, then the appropriate differences among such industries are their independent tendencies to fluctuate over time, as above, but mitigated or amplified by their interrelationships with the other industries in the industry-mix. For this reason, then, not only is it necessary to disaggregate SIC groups far below the durables-nondurables level, it is also necessary to identify the interrelationships among industries that may affect their individual contributions to the level of fluctuations in a given region. It is these "differences" then that are relevant to the analysis here.

The time dimension must also be specified more clearly. Thompson has noted that regional instability may be divided into at least three forms on the basis of the time period with respect to which they apply: short-term or "seasonal" instability, medium-term or "cyclical" instability, and long-term or "growth trend" instability [57, pp. 133-72]. The nature and source of each of these forms of instability or fluctuations is relatively unique, he suggests; and the appropriate policy response will vary from one to another. A region that is diversified with respect to cyclical fluctuations or with respect to longer-term stability in growth trends.

Stability or instability of this last type is a function, according to Thompson, of complementarity in growth trends of the individual industries, that is, a mix of young, mature, and decadent industries [57, p. 162].

"Seasonal" instability in a regional economy refers to relatively easily predictable changes in the utilization of productive capacity that, due to their predictability, "offer a much greater potential for effective intervention [57, p. 163]. "Cyclical" instability, on the other hand, can refer to "a more or less regular oscillation of business activity about a growth trend . . ." [p. 160]. The essential difference between "cyclical" and "seasonal" instability is a function of both predictability and the length of time over which it is manifest. Furthermore, Thompson argues, cyclical fluctuations are the least amenable to local policy initiative. This last conclusion, however, may be in part a reflection of Thompson's pessimism about the potential of local diversification efforts.

If we focus primarily upon this medium-term fluctuation in regional economic activity around its basic trend, the appropriate "differences" among industries are further clarified. They are those differences in independent fluctuations and in interrelationships among industries that are manifest in the medium term around the more pronounced trend.

13

Several further requirements of an ideal diversification index should be specified. The definition of diversification implies an increase in the number of "different" contributing or participating elements or a change in the distribution of a given number of elements in the direction of greater "differences" according to an appropriate criterion. An ideal index of diversification should indicate greater diversification through an increase in the number of elements combined only to the extent that the new elements are appropriately different. A measure that treats all elements as equally different, and, hence, of ostensibly identically diversifying importance, will be appropriate only if the criterion for classifying elements separates them into equally different classes.

The ogive measure and the measure based on deviations from national averages, which are discussed above, would be ideal measures if SIC groupings measured relevant differences with precision and in an equally different fashion, a situation we suggest is improbable. For the case of industrial diversification, an ideal index of diversification will be sensitive to the addition or deletion of an industry at any total number of industries and will be sensitive to the relative magnitude of the differences among industries.

For purposes of evaluating the relative significance of diversified industrial structures, finally, the ideal measure should be independent of all structural characteristics other than the number of industries, their relative weights, and the relevant differences among them. Specifically, it should be independent of city size, growth rate, the total number of industry groups in the classification scheme, and of inappropriate differences among the industries. Any bias of the measure toward such characteristics would preclude the possibility of evaluating their separate relationships to instability and diversification.

In summary, the structural basis of relative regional fluctuations has been studies in this country for nearly half a century. The aura of pessimism about the explanatory power of industry mix is a product of a group of studies that have shown significant relationships but little overall reduction in unexplained variation. Such pessimism may be premature, for the empirical analyses generally cited contained conceptual and empirical difficulties that are very likely to have led to underestimation of the influence of industry mix.

The measures of industrial diversity or diversification proposed to date have also contained conceptual difficulties that limited their usefulness for empirical analysis. An ideal measure of diversification requires careful specification of the objective of diversifying, identification of the appropriate differences among industries, and construction of an index that measures the response in terms of the specified objective to increases in the number of elements combined of different distributions among a given number. Such a measure must be independent of historical and structural characteristics of the subject industrial structures other than those that are specific to diversification.

2

A THEORY OF OPTIMAL REGIONAL INDUSTRIAL DIVERSIFICATION

The concept of industrial diversification, as discussed in Chapter 1, has heretofore lacked a precise specification consistent both with intuitive approaches to the problem and with the mainstream of contemporary economic theory. In this chapter we shall offer a reformulation of the concept that appears to satisfy both requirements to some degree, but neither perfectly.

The analysis that follows consists, in brief, in the application of Markowitz-Tobin "portfolio theory" to the analysis of regional industrial structures. Whereas the Markowitz-Tobin analysis has been developed primarily for theorizing about the allocation of personal financial wealth among alternative financial assets, this study will consider the allocation of real regional resources—the factor resources of the area—among alternative groups of economic activities. Whereas Markowitz and Tobin were concerned with the returns to financial wealth under risk of low or zero financial returns, we shall consider the "returns" that a region derives from its economic activity, such as employment, income, etc., under risk of the instability in such returns that manifests itself over time in fluctuations.

The analysis proceeds in six steps. First the applicability of "portfolio analysis" to the regional industrial structure problem is discussed. Then the problem of dealing with uncertainty in returns is shown to yield, under fairly general conditions, a rationale for diversifying industrial structure in the sense of reducing fluctuations in expected aggregate regional returns. The implications of such "diversification" for the selection of industrial structures is explored at that time. Next the theoretical determination of an optimally diversified industrial structure for a hypothetical single closed regional economy is developed under assumed ideal conditions: complete divisibility of industries, no preexisting industries, and no externalities. It is then demonstrated that in a multiregional context with independent regional industrial structures linked through factor and product flows, the optimally diversified regional structure is identical to the optimally diversified supraregional structure. The relationship between stochastic spatial programming of the type developed here and conventional determinate spatial programming is then established. The basic optimal industrial portfolio selection is reformulated to take into consideration preexisting industries, indivisibilities, alternative technologies, and externalities. Finally, it is shown that this formulation yields a measure of relative industrial diversification that is superior, at least conceptually, to those seen before.

The resulting formulation of the concept of industrial diversification is imperfect in at least two ways. First, the utility theory implicit in the mean-variance analysis in which this formulation is couched has been criticized widely. An appendix to this chapter deals with that problem explicitly and attempts to specify the scope of the qualifications of the results that may be necessary. Second, the empirical validity of the measure of relative industrial diversification derived here is to some extent questionable given the magnitude of the assumptions implicit in its formulation. Chapter 3 of this study is dedicated to the analysis of the empirical validity of the measure. It is concluded there that the new measure derived here is a substantial improvement over those that have been available previously, but again, not a perfect measure.

PORTFOLIO ANALYSIS OF INDUSTRIAL COMPOSITION

The "returns" that an economy derives from the presence of any given industry, however such returns are defined, may be considered essentially stochastic. That is, the returns may be viewed as a random variable with a distinctive probability distribution. Whether such returns consist of income from value-added, employment, prestige, defense, or some weighted subset of these characteristics, they represent benefits to the economy that may be expected to vary with all those exogenous and endogenous characteristics of the economy that affect the rates of production, the factor productivity, and the product mix of the specific industry. Variation of the returns over time, either in terms of growth trends over the longer run or fluctuations around that trend would be captured by the probability distribution on the specific form of return that may be defined.

To the extent that any economy has finite resources capable of generating the returns sought from industry, the utilization of such resources in any specific industry, even for a short period of time, represents an "investment" of those resources in that industry in the financial sense. That is, the economy as a whole has allocated part of its wealth to acquire the services of a productive asset, in this case an industry. Whether undertaken explicitly within a total planning framework or implicitly within a decentralized market framework, the resource allocation may be presumed to take place in the expectation of generating returns from that productive enterprise greater than those obtainable from alternative enterprises, the opportunity costs of the resources.

For those who live in a mixed-market economy such as that of the United States it may be difficult to envision in these terms the process by which new firms or other producing units are formed, staffed, and supplied. We are accustomed to think in terms of firms forming themselves with a labor force eager to be employed and suppliers eager to supply. There seems to be much less freedom to allocate among alternatives than that implied in the discussion above. However, we need only recall that new firms that offer factor payments below the opportunity costs of the factor services sought generally receive no factor services. Furthermore, the eagerness with which Chambers of Commerce and regional development commissions seek new firms for their respective geographical areas is never completely unqualified. The recent upsurge of concern for the environmental impacts of alternative producers is the clearest contemporary example of selective allocation on their part. The historical preference for "electronics" plants because they are environmentally "clean" and because they tend to generate relatively high-wage employment is further evidence.

Given the stochastic nature of the returns to such community allocation of resources, it is rational for those who are evaluating alternative returns to consider not only the expected return (the mean of the probability distribution on returns)[1] but also some measure of the spread of the returns around the mean (say, the variance, standard deviation, or some higher moments). The precise form in which these characteristics will enter the community's objective or criterion function may vary greatly, but so long as there is any aversion to differences in the spread of those returns or to skewness in them, aversion generally associated with the idea of the "risk" involved in stochastic returns, it is rational to assess more than the mean value.[2]

---

1. In an analysis such as this, where stochastic and spatial considerations enter, the use of the word "distribution" tends to recur frequently, but in two contexts. To provide clarity, hereafter the term "distribution on . . ." will be used to refer to the probability distribution of the referenced random variable, and the term "distribution of. . ." will be used to refer to spatial or interpersonal distributions of the referenced variable (not necessarily random).

2. There has arisen an extensive literature with respect to the appropriateness of using only the first two moments of the probability distributions in order to determine which distribution among a set of distributions will in fact dominate the rest. For a review of that literature and a defense of the use of the mean-variance approach in this study, see the Methodological Appendix for this chapter, at the back of the book.

If each industry in an economy may be characterized as an individual community investment, then the set of industries that any given economy has acquired at a point in time may be considered a "portfolio" of community investments among which some or all of the community's economic factor resources are distributed. It has become customary in financial analysis to refer to such sets of stochastic financial assets as an individual's portfolio of securities. It seems appropriate here to refer to the industrial structure of an economy, when viewed stochastically, as the community "industrial portfolio." The nomenclature serves to emphasize not only the stochastic nature of the returns, but also the inherent interdependence among elements of the portfolio that shall be the center of considerable additional discussion below.

If an economy is thus composed of a set of, say J industries, $j = 1, 2, \ldots, J$, each of which may be characterized by "returns" r_j, which are random variables with known expected values, μ_j, and known variances, σ_j^2; and if the returns from the various industries are independently distributed, then following Markowitz [33], a number of interesting properties can be noted for combinations of these industries.

First, the expected return for the whole set or portfolio of J industries among which resources are evenly distributed is given by

$$(2.1) \qquad \mu_p = E(R) = \sum_{j=1}^{J} \mu_j, \text{ where } R = \sum_{j=1}^{J} r_j.$$

The expected value of the average return on industries in the portfolio would be

$$(2.2) \qquad \frac{\mu_p}{J} = E\left(\frac{R}{J}\right) = \frac{\sum_{j=1}^{J} \mu_j}{J}.$$

The variance of the return for the whole set of independent industry returns would be

$$(2.3) \qquad \sigma_p^2 = \text{Var}(R) = \sum_{j=1}^{J} \sigma_j^2.$$

So long as there exists an upper bound, say Z, to the variance of distribution on returns of any industry in the portfolio, then σ_p^2 must be less than or equal to JZ. Now since the variance of the average return per industry would be

$$(2.4) \qquad \frac{\sigma_p^2}{J} = \text{Var}\left(\frac{R}{J}\right) = \left(\frac{1}{J}\right)^2 \sigma_p^2, \text{ and}$$

since σ_p^2 cannot exceed JZ, then

(2.5) $\qquad \dfrac{\sigma_p^2}{J} \leq \left(\dfrac{1}{J}\right)^2 JZ = \dfrac{Z}{J}$,

all by the standard theorems for the variance of sums of uncorrelated random variables.

$\qquad$ Note that as the number of industries in the economy, J, expands, $\dfrac{Z}{J}$ decreases, approaching zero in the limit. In other words if the variances of the individual industry returns have an upper bound (not an unreasonable assumption), the variance of the average of the uncorrelated portfolio approaches zero as the number of industries included in it increases. Sufficient diversification in terms of simply increasing the number of industries, whether specifically pursued or not, would bring under these conditions virtual certainty of return.

$\qquad$ It is, of course, clearly unrealistic to assume that industrial returns are independent of one another. At least two forms of explicit interdependence exist. The first, which we might term production-interdependence, is derived from the interindustry transactions that take place in the production of any given final good. Changes in the level of production of any given final good will affect not only the level of return in the industry class of which that final good is a member but also the level of return in all industries producing intermediate inputs into that final good, even though their industry classifications, based on their final goods, may be different. The second form of interdependence, which we might term consumption-interdependence, is derived from common aspects in the determination of demand for different final goods. Similarities and dissimilarities in the income elasticities of demand for different final goods will establish an interrelationship in the pattern of the returns that their respective producing industries would bring.

$\qquad$ If we relax the assumption of independent distributions on returns, we must deal additionally with the covariances of the individual industry returns. The number of distinct covariances for J random variables, σ_{ij}, not counting variances and not counting σ_{21} as distinct from σ_{12} (that is, the number of distinct off-diagonal elements in the variance-covariance matrix) is equal to $J(J-1)/2$. If we now define the "average covariance," say $\overline{M}$, as the sum of all distinct covariances divided by the number of distinct covariances, we may show that an increase in the number of industries will lead, ceteris paribus, to a reduction of the variance of the average return from the portfolio toward the value of the average covariance.

(2.6) $\qquad \overline{M} = \dfrac{\displaystyle\sum_{j=1}^{J-1} \sum_{i=2}^{J} \sigma_{ij}}{\dfrac{J(J-1)}{2}} = \dfrac{2\displaystyle\sum_{j=1}^{J-1} \sum_{i=2}^{J} \sigma_{ij}}{J(J-1)}$ $\quad$ for all $j < i$, or

(2. 6a)
$$\sum_{j=1}^{J-1} \sum_{i=2}^{J} \sigma_{ij} = \frac{J(J-1)\bar{M}}{2}.$$

Then, when a set of J industries are not independent in their returns, the variance of their unweighted sum is

(2. 7)
$$\hat{\sigma}_p^2 = \sum_i^J \sum_j^J \sigma_{ij}$$

$$= \sum_j^J \sigma_j^2 + 2 \sum_{j=1}^{J-1} \sum_{i=2}^{J} \sigma_{ij} \quad \text{for all } j < i,$$

which is, from (2. 6a)

(2. 8)
$$\hat{\sigma}_p^2 = \sum_j^J \sigma_j^2 + J(J-1)\bar{M}.$$

Similarly, the variance of the average return on an industry in this portfolio is

(2. 9)
$$\frac{\hat{\sigma}_p^2}{J} = \left(\frac{1}{J}\right)^2 \hat{\sigma}_p^2$$

$$= \left(\frac{1}{J}\right)^2 \sum_j^J \sigma_j^2 + J(J-1)\bar{M}$$

$$= \frac{\sum_j^J \sigma_j^2}{J^2} + \frac{J-1}{J}.$$

Note that in (2. 9) the variance of the average return has been separated into two components, the average of the variances of individual industries and the weighted average covariance for the J industries. If, as above, all of the σ_j^2 are bounded from above; then as J increases the first term approaches zero and the coefficient of the second term approaches one. Hence the variance of the average return approaches the average covariance.

This result is due to Markowitz [33, pp. 112-15]. For purposes of evaluating an economy's industrial portfolio, it may be taken to have the following meaning. If a community had an opportunity to invest some of its allocable resources in support of one of two distinct industries and if the two prospective industries had identical expected returns, but one had a variance of those returns considerably greater than the other, the better choice would not necessarily be the less risky of the two on the basis of their respective variances. For the contribution of each to the industrial portfolio variance consists of a contribution to the first term of (2.9), the average of the individual variances plus a contribution to the weighted average covariance among all industries. If the industry with greater variance was, on average, uncorrelated with those of the existing portfolio (or if it had negative covariances with some or all of the existing industries), it could theoretically make a greater contribution to reducing the average portfolio variance than the industry that appeared less risky.

Paraphrasing Markowitz' conclusions with respect to financial securities, the industry that is risky or conservative, appropriate or inappropriate, for one industrial portfolio may be the opposite for another. The returns from any given industry may be highly correlated with those of of some industries but not with those of others. The returns from another industry may have a different, perhaps partially overlapping, pattern of high and low correlations. The problem is to select industries so that their average covariance for a given expected return is small, or so that the trade-off between expected return and the portfolio variance can be made most efficiently. Most important, one must think of selecting an industrial portfolio as a whole, a complete industrial structure, not industries per se.

The analysis until now has assumed that all industries included in the portfolio are of equal size in terms of the proportion of resources allocated to them. Markowitz did not generalize his results to the case where unequal weighting (unequal size) is present. The average portfolio variance from which the critical results above were derived becomes less useful when one is comparing alternative distributions of resources among a given number of industries; for the denominator, based upon the number of industries, would not vary. The value of diversification of industrial structures may also be shown to apply to alternative weighting schemes where any given industry may be from zero to 100 percent of any theoretical portfolio. In this case it is the total portfolio variance, rather than the average, that is the object of minimization efforts. For total portfolio variance can be shown to be a function of the distribution of weights among alternative industries and of the total number of industries. To the extent that a portfolio contains greater proportions of either industries with lower individual variances or industries with low positive or negative average covariance with all other industries, the total portfolio variance, σ_p^2, will be less.

Total portfolio variance, it might be suggested, does not at first appear to be sensitive to larger numbers of or to increases in the number of industries, the most apparent form of diversification. It might be suggested that total specialization in the single industry with the lowest individual variance would minimize the variance. In fact, when the number of industries is not an explicit argument in the function but weights are allowed to vary, the distribution of industries in terms of relative weights will also provide a basis for diversification.

Let us ask specifically what set of weights would minimize σ_p^2. For a given finite universe of, say, J industries, the choice between any subset and an additional industry can be reduced to the problem of choosing between two industries. So let us specify that there exists one industry, i, for which σ_i^2 is a minimum among all industries and another industry, j, which is the next least variable industry and which possesses and expected return identical to that of industry i. The optimal distribution of a portfolio between i and j may be derived analytically by minimizing the portfolio variance where only i and j are allowed to enter. Let

(2.10) $\qquad \sigma_j^2 = \sigma_i^2 + \varepsilon$, where $0 < \varepsilon < \infty$.

The minimization of σ_p^2 proceeds as follows:

(2.11) $\qquad \sigma_p^2 = w_i^2 \sigma_i^2 + (1 - w_i)^2 (\sigma_i^2 + \varepsilon) + 2w_i (1 - w_i) \sigma_{ij}$

where σ_{ij} is the covariance between i and j. Expanding, simplifying, and taking the derivative with respect to w_i, we have,

(2.12) $\qquad \sigma_p^2 = 2w_i^2 \sigma_i^2 + \sigma_i^2 - 2w_i\sigma_i^2 + \varepsilon + w_i^2 \varepsilon - 2w_i\varepsilon$

$\qquad\qquad + 2w_i\sigma_{ij} - 2w_i^2\sigma_{ij}$

(2.12a) $\qquad \dfrac{d\sigma_p^2}{dw_i} = 4w_i\sigma_i^2 - 2\sigma_i^2 + 2w_i\varepsilon - 2\varepsilon + 2\sigma_{ij} - 4w_i\sigma_{ij}.$

And by setting (2.12a) equal to zero and solving for w_i^*, we obtain

(2.12b) $\qquad w_i^* = \dfrac{\sigma_i^2 + \varepsilon - \sigma_{ij}}{2\sigma_i^2 + \varepsilon - 2\sigma_{ij}}$

$\qquad\qquad\quad = \dfrac{\sigma_j^2 - \sigma_{ij}}{\sigma_i^2 + \sigma_j^2 - 2\sigma_{ij}}$ from (2.10).

The interpretation of (2.12b) is clearest if we consider three distinct cases, $\sigma_{ij} = 0$, $\sigma_{ij} > 0$, and $\sigma_{ij} < 0$. In the first case, i and j uncorrelated, the optimal proportion to be placed in the least variable industry (i) is equal to the ratio of the variance of the more varible industry to the sum of the two variances. Now since σ_j^2 is greater than σ_i^2 from (2.10), in this case the greater the difference between σ_i^2 and σ_j^2 (that is, the greater the value of ε) the larger the proportion of the portfolio dedicated to the less variable industry. If ε is bounded from above, however, w_i^* will not reach 1.0. Some portion of industry j would be included in this industrial portfolio no matter how large its (finite) variance. On the other hand, with $\sigma_{ij} = 0$, as the value of ϵ approached zero the value of w_i^* would approach $\frac{1}{2}$. The maximum optimal proportion for either of the two uncorrelated industries would be $\frac{1}{2}$.

If the two industries have positive covariance, $\sigma_{ij} > 0$, the value of w_i^* will be adjusted for that fact. For a given ϵ and any positive value of σ_{ij}, the numerator of (2.12b) will be reduced by that quantity, the denominator will be reduced by twice that quantity, and w_i^* will be larger than in the comparable uncorrelated case. In the extreme, if σ_{ij} exceeds σ_i^2, then w_i^* would attempt to become greater than one.[3] The effective meaning, of course, is that industry j would not be included in the portfolio. Thus complete specialization in one of two industries with identical means would take place only where the positive covariance between the two candidate industries is greater than the individual variance of the less variable industry.

On the other hand, if σ_{ij} is a negative quantity, the numerator will be increased by twice that quantity, and hence for any value of ϵ, w_j^* will be greater than that which corresponded to the uncorrelated case. And here also as the value of ϵ approaches zero, the optimal share approaches $\frac{1}{2}$.

We are thus able to conclude that where the total number of industries is relatively small and differences in industrial portfolios are manifest solely in different distributions of total resources among that set of industries, changes in the relative concentration can reduce the total portfolio variance in a manner strictly analogous to the effect upon the average portfolio variance from increasing the number of industries included in the portfolio.

AN OPTIMAL REGIONAL INDUSTRIAL PORTFOLIO

Expected returns from different industrial structures cannot realistically be considered identical. We proceed now to the identification of optimal industrial portfolios where both returns and variances vary among prospective industry mixes.

---

3. This is an independent proof of and an extension of the point made by Samuelson [50, pp. 6-7]. It follows from (2.12b) that

$$\frac{\sigma_j^2 - \sigma_{ij}}{\sigma_i^2 + \sigma_j^2 - 2\sigma_{ij}} > 1 \text{ when } \sigma_j^2 - \sigma_{ij} > \sigma_i^2 + \sigma_j^2 - 2\sigma_{ij}, \text{ or } \sigma_{ij} > \sigma_i^2.$$

And by decomposing σ_{ij} into $\rho\sigma_i\sigma_j$ where ρ denotes the Pearson correlation coefficient and σ_i and σ_j denote the respective standard deviations, we obtain $w_i^* > 1$, when $\rho > \sigma_i/\sigma_j$, which concurs with Sharpe [51, p. 138].

Let us assume that there exists a single closed economic region that possesses a fixed quantity of known human and nonhuman resources, that all resources are perfectly mobile within the region and perfectly immobile across regional boundaries, and that we begin with a tabula rasa with respect to industries in the region. Assume further that there exists a set of industries, each of which is capable of producing in the given region if resources are made available to it in the appropriate amounts. Assume, finally, that each industry is infinitely divisible into plants of different scale.

Let the returns to the H different resources, $h = 1, 2, \ldots, H$, of the region from each of the industries be known only stochastically, and let the risk-averse policy makers be concerned with only the first two moments of the respective distributions on returns to the various factors from the various industries. The optimal allocation of the region's resources among alternative uses under these idealized conditions will prove, with one further simplification, to be a case in which the straight-forward application of classical Markowitz-Tobin portfolio analysis is possible. The gradual relaxation of the least appropriate assumptions will generate a set of specific extensions of that analysis, which, it is believed, will prove more useful for the problem at hand.

Let x_{hj} be the proportion of resource h allocated to production in industry j; and let μ_{hj} be the expected value of the index of returns per unit of resource h invested in industry j. Then total returns to a region, with b_h total quantity of each resource h, to be derived from any portfolio in which all resources are allocated to one industry or another will be

$$(2.13) \qquad \mu_p = \sum_h^H \sum_j^J x_{hj}\, \mu_{hj}\, b_h, \text{ where}$$

$$(2.13a) \qquad \sum_j^J x_{hj} = 1 \text{ for all } h,$$

$$(2.13b) \qquad 0 \le x_{hj} \le 1 \text{ for all } h \text{ and } j, \text{ and}$$

$$(2.13c) \qquad 0 \le b_h \le \infty \text{ for all } h.$$

Classical portfolio analysis has been developed in terms of unidimensional resources, generally investible funds. For reasons of comparability and computational convenience, we can reduce the multiresource case to a single dimension in the following way. Let

$$(2.14) \qquad x_j = \frac{\sum_h^H x_{hj}}{H} \text{ and } \mu_j = \frac{\sum_h^H \mu_{hj}}{H}.$$

24

That is, x_j is the proportion of a standardized unit of available resources allocated to industry j, and μ_j is expected return to the region per unit of such standardized resources. For interregional comparisons, as we shall note below, both the composition of the standard resource unit and the returns to be derived per unit in each region from each industry will vary. This will reflect both the relative resource endowments and locational characteristics of production and transport of products.

Total expected return from the industrial portfolio per unit of standardized resources may now be expressed as[4]

(2.15) $\qquad \mu_p = \sum_j x_j \mu_j$, where

(2.15a) $\qquad \sum_j^J x_j = 1$, and

(2.15b) $\qquad 0 \leq x_j \leq 1$ for all j.

In this latter formulation we have deliberately omitted an expression for the total quantity of resources available for investment. Such is possible by virtue of the assumed infinite divisibility of all industries combined with the "separation theorem" of Tobin [60], which notes that under such conditions the optimal solution is independent of the quantity of investable resources.

If each industry is infinitely divisible, then the total number of possible combinations of industries, the number of theoretically possible portfolios, is multiply infinite. Each such portfolio that is evaluated solely in terms of its mean value and variance may be represented graphically by a single point in a mean value-variance space such as that of Figure 2.1. Given limited resources, there is a finite limit to the total portfolio expected return that a region can obtain from industries. And given an upper bound on individual variances and an upper and lower bound on covariances, all portfolios that are "feasible" in

---

4. The correspondence between (2.13a) and 2.15a) can be established as follows:

$$\sum_j^J x_j = \sum_j^J \frac{\sum_h^H x_{hj}}{H} \text{ from (2.14),} = \frac{1}{H} \sum_j^J \sum_h^H x_{hj} = \frac{1}{H} \sum_h^H \sum_j^J x_{kj}$$

$$= \frac{1}{H} \sum_h^H (1) = 1 \text{ from (2.13a).}$$

FIGURE 2.1

Mean-Variance Space and the Efficiency Frontier

(infinite asset divisibility assumed)

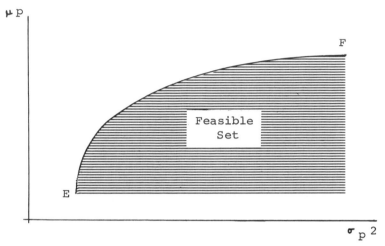

the sense of fulfilling the relevant constraints will appear in the qua-
drant shown in Figure 2.1 and will be bounded by a continuous, convex
curve in the figure labeled EF for "efficiency frontier" [33]. The portfolios represented by points along the efficiency frontier are said to be
"efficient" in that no other portfolio possessing the same expected
return has a smaller variance; or, conversely, no other portfolio possessing identical variance has a greater expected return.

Sharpe has demonstrated that the efficiency frontier can be derived
by minimizing the following linear function of the two parameters (a
quadratic function of x_j) for all values of λ (the slope) from 0 to ∞ [52].

(2.16) $\text{Min } \phi = -\lambda \mu_p + \sigma_p^2$

$$= -\lambda \left(\sum_j x_j \mu_j \right) + \sum_i \sum_j \sigma_{ij}$$

subject to (2.15a and b) and any other linear constraints on feasibility.

This efficiency frontier is in fact a risk-return transformation curve.
For along its length additional return may be achieved only at the cost
of additional risk.

The identification of the single optimal portfolio from among the
single infinity of points in the efficiency frontier requires the superimposition of a community risk indifference function. Let us assume that
there exists for the region we have been considering a single planner

or planning board or other decision maker to whom responsibility has been delegated for choosing the industrial structure. Let us assume further that this representative of the community perceives that the community is, on the whole, averse to risk. More precisely, given a choice between an industry that would produce $100,000 in local income per year with certainty and an industry that would produce $150,000 per year with probability .5 and $50,000 with probability .5, the community would choose the former.

Risk aversion may enter the community utility function in many forms. For the sake of simplicity let us assume that for the given region the utility function is a linear function of the expected return and the variance such that the slope is always greater than zero. That is,

(2.17) $\qquad U = \mu_p - (\gamma)\sigma_p^2$

where γ is the slope of the risk indifference function and is also referred to as the risk-aversion parameter and where the signs are assumed as given and where $\delta u/\delta\mu > 0$, $\delta u/\delta\sigma_p^2 < 0$. The greater the value of γ the greater the (negative) weight placed on the variance in the utility function. The risk aversion of any specific community may be represented by specific values of γ, say γ^0.

FIGURE 2.2

Linear Risk Indifference Map
and the Efficiency Frontier

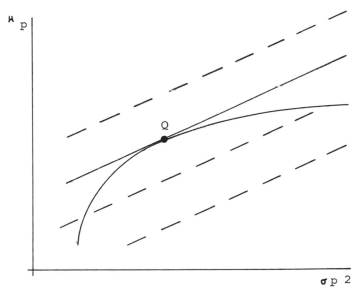

Figure 2.2 shows the superimposition of a linear risk-indifference map with $\gamma^0 = \frac{1}{2}$. The tangency between the risk indifference curve (I_3) and the efficiency frontier identifies the coordinates (and the composition) of the optimal portfolio for the region. This is the portfolio (Q in Figure 2.2) for which the marginal rate of substitution of risk for return along the indifference curve equals the marginal rate of transformation of risk into return along the region's efficiency frontier.

The determination of the optimal portfolio may be accomplished in this case through the maximization of the regional utility function.

(2.18) $\text{Max } U = \mu_p - \gamma \sigma_p^2$

$$= \sum_j x_j \mu_j - \gamma \sum_i \sum_j x_i x_j \sigma_{ij}.$$

In matrix form, this becomes

(2.18')

$$\text{Max } U = \begin{bmatrix} \mu_1 \\ \mu_2 \\ \cdot \\ \cdot \\ \cdot \\ \cdot \\ \cdot \\ \cdot \\ \mu_j \end{bmatrix} \Bigg/ \begin{bmatrix} x_1 \\ x_2 \\ \cdot \\ \cdot \\ \cdot \\ \cdot \\ \cdot \\ \cdot \\ x_j \end{bmatrix} - \gamma \begin{bmatrix} x_1 \\ x_2 \\ \cdot \\ \cdot \\ \cdot \\ \cdot \\ \cdot \\ \cdot \\ x_j \end{bmatrix} \Bigg/ \begin{bmatrix} \sigma_1^2 & \sigma_{12} & \sigma_{13} \cdots \cdots \cdots \cdots & \sigma_{1j} \\ \sigma_{21} & \sigma_2^2 & \sigma_{23} \cdots \cdots \cdots \cdots & \sigma_{2j} \\ \sigma_{31} & & & \cdot \\ \cdot & & & \cdot \\ \cdot & & & \cdot \\ \cdot & & & \cdot \\ & & & \sigma_{(i-1)j} \\ \sigma_{i1} \cdots \cdots \cdots \cdots \sigma_{i(j-1)} \sigma_j^2 \end{bmatrix} \begin{bmatrix} x_1 \\ x_2 \\ \cdot \\ \cdot \\ \cdot \\ \cdot \\ \cdot \\ \cdot \\ x_j \end{bmatrix}$$

$$= \mu'x - \lambda x' \sum x$$

subject to

(2.18a) $\sum_j x_j = 1$ and $x_j \geq 0$.

The optimal portfolio, Q, will contain that set of industries that yields the optimal trade-off between expected return for the entire portfolio and the variance of the distribution on returns from the entire portfolio. It will be the optimally diversified portfolio in that it contains the number of "appropriately different" industries that will minimize the variance for the respective level of return. It will also provide the optimally specialized industrial structure. For the value of μ_j incorporated in the calculation of μ_p presumably incorporates all of the potential returns associated with specialization. Given the utility function of the region, no further specialization was appropriate because of the costs of increased variability (from movement along the efficiency frontier) or decreased efficiency (from movement inside the frontier), which additional specilization would entail.[5]

INTERREGIONALLY OPTIMAL INDUSTRIAL PORTFOLIOS

The relationships between location of markets, location of production inputs, and the cost of transport of both inputs and products are such that it would be highly unlikely for any industry that produces for a market area larger than the region within which it is located to produce identical returns to factors occurring in varying proportions among regions in a supraregional area. The nature of the advantages of specialization and production of goods and services on the basis of dynamic comparative advantage provide further intuitive support for a suggestion that the returns to be derived from a given industry will vary across regions. The only context where this supposition would be likely to fail is one in which perfect factor substitutability is encountered.

The selection of optimal portfolios for individual regions in a multiregional context thus consists of a process of relating individual regional resource stocks to their different respective regional feasibility sets and efficiency frontiers. In this context one may ask, What relationship exists between the optimal industrial structure for the individual regions and the maximization of utility for the supraregional area as a whole? It can be shown that under free trade between component regions and with or without factor mobility the conventional conclusions of trade theory hold. The optimal (and optimally diversified) industrial structure for a component region from its own point of view is identical with that appropriate for the supraregional entity so long as the criterion utility function is identical among individual regions and, hence, identical in consensus.

Consider first the case of two contiguous regions, A and B, that possess different sets of factor stocks and, as a consequence, different markets for factors and products. Assume that products move freely across the interregional boundary, but that factors do not. Let the joint objective be the maximization of total utility for the two regions according to a common utility function of the linearly risk-averse form of equation (2.17). For two regions, it would be as follows:

---

5. As formulated here the returns to investment of regional resources are independent of scale in the various industries. No "gains from specialization" associated with scale or associated with economies external to the individual industries are incorporated explicitly. But for a process for incorporating them explicitly, see page 42.

(2.19) $\quad U^{A+B} = \mu_p{}^A + \mu_p{}^B - \gamma[(\sigma_p{}^2)^A + (\sigma_p{}^2)^B]$

or in expanded form, assuming a common universe of industries from which to choose,

$$(2.20) \quad U^{A+B} = \sum_j^J x_j{}^A \mu_j{}^A + \sum_j^J x_j{}^B \mu_j{}^B - \gamma\left(\sum_i^J \sum_j^J x_i{}^A x_j{}^A \sigma_{ij}{}^A \right.$$

$$\left. + \sum_i^J \sum_j^J x_i{}^B x_j{}^B \sigma_{ij}{}^B\right)$$

where $x_j{}^A$, $\mu_j{}^A$, and $\sigma_{ij}{}^A$ have the same meaning as their unsuperscripted variants in equation (2.14). In matrix form, this becomes

(2.21)

$$U^{A+B} = \begin{bmatrix} \mu_1{}^A \\ \mu_2{}^A \\ \cdot \\ \cdot \\ \cdot \\ \mu_J{}^A \\ \mu_1{}^B \\ \mu_2{}^B \\ \cdot \\ \cdot \\ \cdot \\ \mu_J{}^B \end{bmatrix}' \begin{bmatrix} x_1{}^A \\ x_2{}^A \\ \cdot \\ \cdot \\ \cdot \\ x_J{}^A \\ x_1{}^B \\ x_2{}^B \\ \cdot \\ \cdot \\ \cdot \\ x_J{}^B \end{bmatrix} - \gamma \begin{bmatrix} x_1{}^A \\ x_2{}^A \\ \cdot \\ \cdot \\ \cdot \\ x_J{}^A \\ x_1{}^B \\ x_2{}^B \\ \cdot \\ \cdot \\ \cdot \\ x_J{}^B \end{bmatrix}' \begin{bmatrix} (\sigma_1{}^2)^A & \sigma_{12}{}^A & \cdots & \sigma_{1j}{}^A \\ \sigma_{21}{}^A & (\sigma_2{}^2)^A & \cdot & \\ \cdot & & \cdot & \\ \cdot & & & \cdot \\ (\sigma_{J1}{}^A) & \cdots & & (\sigma_j{}^2)^A \\ (\sigma_1{}^2)^B & \sigma_{12}{}^B & \cdots & \sigma_{1J}{}^B \\ \sigma_{21}{}^B & (\sigma_2{}^2)^B & \cdot & \\ \cdot & & \cdot & \\ \sigma_{J1}{}^B & & & (\sigma_J{}^2)^B \end{bmatrix} \begin{bmatrix} x_1{}^A \\ x_2{}^A \\ \cdot \\ \cdot \\ \cdot \\ x_J{}^A \\ x_1{}^B \\ x_2{}^B \\ \cdot \\ \cdot \\ \cdot \\ x_J{}^B \end{bmatrix}$$

$$= \hat{\mu}'\hat{x} - \gamma\,\hat{x}'\,\hat{\Sigma}\,\hat{x}.$$

If region A in this pair of regions were to proceed to maximize its separate utility given this utility function and the constraint that $\sum_j x_j{}^A = 1$, the optimal industrial structure would be identified completely by the values of all $x_j{}^A$. Let us reduce the problem by suggesting that there exist only two industries, 1 and 2, in the universe from which regions A and B may choose. The optimal portfolio will be identified by means of the relative weights given to these two industries. Assuming that A participates in the same trade relationship with B whether it is pursuing its own welfare or their joint welfare, the vector of returns to factors in A from different industries may be considered the same in both cases. The specific maximization problem for the single region is the following:

(2.22) $\text{Max } f(U^A) = x_1^A \mu_1^A + x_2^A \mu_2^A - \gamma^0 2x_1^A x_{12}^A - \gamma^0 (x_1^A)^2 \sigma_{11}^A$

$\qquad\qquad - \gamma^0 (x_2^A)^2 \sigma_{22}^A - \gamma^0 2x_1^A x_2^A \sigma_{12}^A$

S.T. $g(x_1, x_2) = x_1 + x_2 = 1.$

By forming the Lagrangian of this maximum problem and solving the Kuhn-Tucker conditions for x_1^A, x_2^A, and λ^A (the Lagrangian multiplier) we can determine the values of all three variables associated with the optimal portfolio from the point of view of region A alone.

The Kuhn-Tucker conditions for (2.22) are

(2.23a) $\dfrac{\delta f}{\delta x_1^A} - \lambda^A \dfrac{\delta g}{\delta x_1^A} = \mu_1^A - 2\gamma^0 x_2^A \sigma_{12}^A - 2x_{11}^A - \lambda^A = 0$

(2.23b) $\dfrac{\delta f}{\delta x_2^A} - \lambda^A \dfrac{\delta g}{\delta x_2^A} = \mu_2^A - 2\gamma^0 x_1^A \sigma_{12}^A - 2x_2^A \sigma_{22}^A - \lambda^A = 0$

(2.23c) $\lambda_g^A (x_1^A, x_2^A) = \lambda^A x_1^A + \lambda^A x_2^A - \lambda^A = 0$

(2.23d) $g(x_1^A, x_2^A) \geq 0 = x_1^A + x_2^A = 1$

(2.23e) $\lambda^A \geq 0.$

Equations (2.23a), (2.23b), and (2.23c) form a system of three simultaneous equations in three unknowns (x_1^A, x_2^A and λ^A) and, there-fore, solution of them will yield unique values of the variables. Given the concavity of the criterion function and the linearity (convexity) of the constraint, the Kuhn-Tucker derived values of these variables will provide necessary and sufficient conditions for a unique maximum. The actual analytical solutions in terms of parameters in this case yield rather complex terms from which it is not possible to demonstrate ana-lytically that conditions (2.23d) and (2.23e) are met. Fortunately, we may establish the point in question without such conditions.

To do so, we note that the maximization of the joint utility of the two regions, under the assumption of just two industries, consists of the following problem:

(2.24) $\underset{x}{\text{Max}}\ f(U^{A+B}) = x_1^A \mu_1^A + x_1^B \mu_1^B + x_2^A \mu_2^A + x_2^B \mu_2^B$

$$- \gamma^0 [2x_1^A x_2^A \sigma_{ij} + (x_1^A)^2 \sigma_{11}^A + (x_2^A)^2 \sigma_{22}^A]$$

$$- \gamma^0 [2x_1^B x_2^B \sigma_{ij}^B + (x_1^B)^2 \sigma_{11}^B + (x_2^B)^2 \sigma_{22}^B]$$

S.T. $g^A(x_1^A, x_2^A) = x_1^A + x_2^A = 1$

and $g^B(x_1^B, x_2^B) = x_1^B + x_2^B = 1.$

The Kuhn-Tucker conditions for this problem are as follows:

(2.25a) $\dfrac{\delta f}{\delta x_1^A} - \lambda^A \dfrac{\delta g^A}{\delta x_1^A} - \lambda^B \dfrac{\delta g^B}{\delta x_1^A} = \mu_1^A + 2\gamma^0 \sigma_{12}^A - 2\gamma^0 x_1^A \sigma_{11}^A - \lambda^A = 0$

(2.25b) $\dfrac{\delta f}{\delta x_1^B} - \lambda^A \dfrac{\delta g^A}{\delta x_1^B} - \lambda^B \dfrac{\delta g^B}{\delta x_1^B} = \mu_1^B + 2\gamma^0 \sigma_{12}^B - 2\gamma^0 x_1^B \sigma_{11}^B - \lambda^B = 0$

(2.25c) $\dfrac{\delta f}{\delta x_2^A} - \lambda^A \dfrac{\delta g^A}{\delta x_2^A} - \lambda^B \dfrac{\delta g^B}{\delta x_2^A} = \mu_2^B + 2\gamma^0 \sigma_{12}^A - 2\gamma^0 x_2^A \sigma_{22}^A - \lambda^A = 0$

(2.25d) $\dfrac{\delta f}{\delta x_2^B} - \lambda^A \dfrac{\delta g^A}{\delta x_2^B} - \lambda \dfrac{B \delta g^B}{\delta x_2^B} = \mu_2^B + 2\gamma^0 \sigma_{12}^B - 2\gamma^0 x_2^B \sigma_{22}^B - \lambda^B = 0$

(2.25e) $\lambda^A g^A (x_1^A, x_2^A) = \lambda^A x_1^A + \lambda^A x_2^A - \lambda^A = 0$

(2.25f) $\lambda^B x^B (x_1^B, x_2^B) = \lambda^B x_1^B + \lambda^B x_2^B - \lambda^B = 0$

(2.25g) $g^A (x_1^A, x_2^A) \geq 0 = x_1^A + x_2^A = 1$

(2.25h) $g^B (x_1^B, x_2^B) \geq 0 = x_1^B + x_2^B = 1$

(2.25i) and (2.25j) λ^A and $\lambda^B \geq 0.$

Now it is readily apparent that equations (2.25a) through (2.25f) form a system of six equations in six unknowns (x_1^A, x_2^A, x_1^B, x_2^B, λ^A and

λ^B) that can be solved to determine the values of the variables that are optimal from a supraregional viewpoint. But it is also true that equations (2.25a), (2.25c), and (2.25e) form a system of three equations in the three unknowns for region A, that these three unknowns appear nowhere else in the larger system, and that the equations in which they occur are identical to those of equations (2.23a) through (2.23c). It is, therefore, trivially apparent that the optimal values of x_1^A, x_2^A, and λ^A are identical in both cases. Without needing to solve for specific values we know that if a solution exists in the first case, then the regionally optimal industrial structure is also supraregionally optimal.

These results may be generalized considerably. First, the extension from two industries in each region to any finite n industries or the extension from two regions to any finite m regions are both straightforward extensions that will not alter the results. Second, the constraint set may be expanded arbitrarily so long as it remains linear and regionally independent throughout. Introduction of interdependence in the constraints, such as one involving common resources (for example, airsheds or watersheds) will alter the results.

The interregional independence of industrial structures assumed here is actually a more severe constraint than it may seem to appear at first. It implies, for example, that the rates of return to factor resources among regions are independent. That is, the return to region A from industry one is independent of rates of production in that same industry in region B, even if they are contiguous free-trade partners. It is no more restrictive, however, than the other constraints implicit in linear spatial programming models, for example, given prices for all final goods in all regions.

Finally, factor mobility may be introduced by creating a factor-supply industry (involving transport and transformation) and by expressing all returns in per capita terms. Resources would be allocated to such an industry only when the returns from such exceed all alternatives; and, conceptually, migration would take place only then.

OPTIMAL INDUSTRIAL STRUCTURES
AND CONVENTIONAL SPATIAL PROGRAMMING

The industrial portfolio model may be related directly to previous determinate models of regional and interregional programming such as the linear single-region programming formulations of Isard [23] and the linear multiregion formulations of Takayama and Judge (56), which permit and program interregional flows. Two principal differences appear. First, in the portfolio model a large proportion of the information generally included in the constraint set is incorporated directly into the criterion function. Second, the portfolio model utilizes the parameters of probability distributions on the fixed coefficients of the maximand rather than assuming that they are determinate. The portfolio model, as presented here, is in fact a simple stochastic extension of basic linear spatial programming.

Consider the model discussed by Isard [23, pp. 448-60]. For a hypothetical isolated single region, he postulates that there exist n possible activities for achieving regional income and m possible constraints that reflect fixed supplies of resources available. Assuming that the prices of finished products are given, the linear program for maximizing regional income is to maximize:

$$(2.26) \qquad f(Y) = \sum_{j}^{n} c_j q_j$$

subject to

$$(2.26a) \qquad \sum_{h}^{m} \sum_{j}^{n} a_{hj} q_j \leq b_h$$

$$(2.26b) \qquad q_j \geq 0 \text{ for all } j$$

where a_{hj} denotes the given number of units of input factor h required per unit of output in industry j;

c_j denotes the given per-unit level of income to be derived with certainty from activity j;

q_j denotes the variable quantity of output in industry j; and

b_h denotes the given total supply of factor h available in the region.

The problem in this form should be compared with maximizing equation (2.13), the total expected return from the industrial structure of a single region:

$$(2.13) \qquad \mu_p = \sum_{h} \sum_{j} x_{hj} \mu_{hj}$$

subject to

$$(2.13a) \qquad \sum_{j} x_{hj} \leq 1$$

$$(2.13b) \qquad x_{hj} \geq 0$$

where μ_{hj} was defined as the expected return per unit of resource h from allocation to industry j; and

x_{hj} was defined as the proportion of total available resource h allocated to production in industry j.

The equivalence of the two approaches can be established directly. If the information required in the program, the set of restrictive conditions, and the functional form are identical, then the maximim problems are identical. Note first that the information contained in x_{hj} is identical to that of the constraint set (2.26a). By definition,

$$(2.27) \qquad x_{hj} = \frac{a_{hj}}{b_h} q_j.$$

The restrictive conditions implied by (2.26a), that demand for factor inputs not exceed supply, is met by the equivalent condition that the sum of the factor proportions allocated not exceed one for all resources. For as can be seen readily, (2.26a) may also be expressed as

$$(2.28) \qquad \frac{\sum\limits_{j} a_{hj} q_j}{b_h} \leq 1$$

and from (2.27), this is identical to (2.13a),

$$(2.29) \qquad \sum\limits_{j} x_{hj} = \frac{\sum\limits_{j} a_{hj} q_j}{b_h} \leq 1.$$

Finally, if c_j is disaggregated into its individual factor-return components, that is $c_j = (1/H) \Sigma_h^H c_{hj}$, and considered to be stochastic rather than determinate, it proves to be identical to $\mu_j = (1/H) \Sigma_h^H \mu_{hj}$ from equation (2.14). The income per unit of productive activity is thus the determinate counterpart of mean expected return per unit of resources allocated to that activity under uncertainty.

Equation (2.13) was the first-order portion of the quadratic function that we maximized in equation (2.18). The second-order portion of (2.18) was merely the weighted risk penalty consisting of the variance corresponding to the first term, weighted by the variable risk-aversion parameter. In general, as shown by Mandansky [31], any determinate linear programming problem will become a quadratic programming problem under uncertainty with respect to the fixed coefficients of the objective function, so long as the first two moments of the probability distributions on those coefficients are considered to incorporate all of the relevant information.

The interregional programming variant of the portfolio model may be similarly related to determinate linear models in the literature. Consider, for example, a simplified version of one model presented by Takayama and Judge [56, pp. 25-28]. They offer a "net revenue maximizing" formulation of interregional spatial equilibrium. By altering their notation to conform to the conventions used here (products or industries subscripted, regions superscripted) and by omitting primary and intermediate commodity flows, their model may be presented as follows:

Given pairs of regions ℓ and k (ℓ, k = 1, . . . K) producing and shipping products j (j = 1, . . . J) with immobile factor resources h (h = 1, ... H), the problem is to maximize the net value of final product across all regions. That is, to maximize,

(2.30)
$$f(x) = \sum_k \sum_j p_j^k q_j^{\ell k} - \sum_\ell \sum_k \sum_j t_j^{\ell k} q_j^{\ell k} - \sum_\ell \sum_j c_j^\ell q_j^\ell$$

$$= \sum_\ell \sum_k \sum_j (p_j^k - t_j^{\ell k}) q_j^{\ell k} - \sum_\ell \sum_j c_j^\ell q_j^\ell$$

subject to

(2.30a) $q_j^\ell - \sum_k q_j^{\ell k} \overset{\geq}{=} 0$ for all j;

(2.30b) $s_h^k - \sum_j a_{hj}^k q_j^k \geq 0$ for all h; and

(2.30c) $q_j^k, q_j^{k\ell} \overset{\geq}{=} 0$ for all k and j

where p_j^k denotes the predetermined final product price for product j in region k;

$q_j^{\ell k}$ denotes the variable quantity of a final product; shipped between regions ℓ and k;

$t_j^{\ell k}$ denotes the unit transport cost for a shipment of a final commodity from region i to j, independent of volume or direction;

c_j^ℓ denotes the unit plant costs of producing a final product j in region ℓ, assumed independent of the scale of production;

q_j^ℓ denotes the level of production of a final product j in region ℓ;

s_h^k denotes the given quantity of immobile primary commodity (resource) h in region k; and

a_{hj}^k denotes the (constant proportional) rate at which primary commodity h is required for production of product j.

Constraint set (2.30a) is the requirement that outshipments programmed not exceed production programmed for any region, and (2.30b) corresponds to (2.26a).

If we let $q_j^{\ell k}$ in equation (2.30) refer to production in region ℓ <u>and</u> flow to all regions (including flows to itself, denoted $q^{\ell \ell}$, where implicitly $q_j^{\ell \ell} = q_j^\ell - \sum_k q_j^{\ell k}$ and $t_j^{\ell \ell} = 0$) then equation (2.30) may be rewritten

36

(2.31) $f(x) = \sum_\ell \sum_k \sum_j (p_j^\ell - c_j^k - t_j^{k\ell}) q_j^{k\ell}.$

The term within parentheses on the right-hand side represents net revenue per unit of output of product j.

In the portfolio model we have dealt with returns of a generally unspecified nature from industries implicitly capable of producing a set of products. If we assume that each industry in the model produces a single final product comparable to products in the Takayama and Judge model and that the "return" to a given region is to be defined as "net revenue" from production, then the total returns to a region k from an industry j may be specified in the notation of Takayama and Judge as

(2.32) $r_j^k = \sum_\ell (p_j^\ell - c_j^k - t_j^{k\ell}) q_j^{k\ell}.$

That is, return is equal to the net revenue from production and sale of product j to all regions including the region within which the plant is located (that is, where $\ell = k$).

If that return is uncertain, due to uncertainty in either costs of production and transport or to levels of demand, then specification of r_j^k in terms of its expected value, μ_j^k, is an appropriate extension.

As in (?. ?7) and (2. 38) above, the full information and constraint conditions of constraints (2. 30b) are contained in the specification of x_{hj} and x_j of the portfolio model. And since the portfolio model is specified in terms of total production levels rather than in terms of interregional flows, constraints (2. 30a) are superfluous. Once again we see that if we were to substitute (2. 33) into (2. 31) and introduce an expression for the magnitude of the second moment as a risk penalty, then the formulation would be equivalent to the quadratic expansion of the Takayama and Judge model as a result of the introduction of uncertainty.

THE TREATMENT OF PREEXISTING INDUSTRIES, INDIVISIBILITIES, AND EXTERNALITIES

The choice of industries for an industrial portfolio differs from the choice of securities in a number of significant ways. In the first place, whereas a portfolio of securities is theoretically subject to complete turnover at each reevaluation (all currently held securities may be sold and a totally new portfolio created), there exist substantial regidities in the industrial composition of an economy because of the durability and immobility of real capital, the relative weakness of markets for second-hand real capital, and the high costs of converting from one product or product-line to another (except within very narrow ranges).

We have been assuming that there were no previously existing industries in any of the regions for which optimal industrial structures were being derived. The relaxation of that assumption places us in the context of deriving optimal changes in a given industrial structure where some constraints upon the magnitude of decreases in existing industries may be desirable.

This task can be accomplished most directly by means of a set of linear constraints on values of x_j^k, the proportion of resources allocated to industry j in region k, where $j = 1, 2, \ldots g, g + 1, \ldots, J$ and where we are now concerned with the g preexisting industries out of the potential universe of J industries. The specific form of such constraints will depend upon the manner in which the planner wishes to treat individual preexisting industries. Several basic forms of treatment are possible, with many additional combinations of these forms also possible:

1. If it is desired to maintain all preexisting industries at prior absolute levels of production and to add only new (different) industries, as would be consistent with diversifying a set of independent industries, then an equality constraint of the following form might be used:

$$(2.33) \qquad x_j^k = (1 + d_j^k) \, b_j^k$$

where b_j^k denotes the proportion of resources allocated to j in k during the preceding period relative to total resources to be allocated in that regions in this period;[6] and

d_j^k denotes the rate of depreciation of depreciable assets of j in k.

Thus, maintenance of absolute levels requires only the additional allocation of resources to cover depreciation.

2. If it is desired to enforce a predetermined reduction in activity in an industry, the constraint would be of the form:

$$(2.34) \qquad x_j^k = (\eta_j^k + d_j^k) \, b_j^k$$

---

6. That is, if $e_j^k{}_{(t-1)}$ is the absolute quantity of last period resources allocated to j in k, and if total resources in this period are given by H_t^k, then

$$b_t^k = \frac{e_j^k{}_{(t-1)}}{H_t^k}$$

If $H_{t-1}^k = H_t^k$ (no increase in total resources), then neither the absolute nor the relative share of resources allocated to j in k will change.

where $0 \leq \eta_j^k < 1$, and η_j^k denotes that rate of change in activity.

3. Similarly, a predetermined increase in activity in an industry could be programmed through a constraint of the form:

$$(2.35) \qquad x_j^k = (\eta_j^k + d_j^k) \, b_j^k$$

where $1 < \eta_j^k < \infty$.

4. Greater reliance upon the optimizing procedure within the programming framework could be accomplished by specifying minimum activity levels (maximum activity reduction levels) and by permitting that reductions take place only when optimal within the total program. This would require an inequality constraint such as:

$$(2.36) \qquad x_j^k \geq (\eta_j^k + d_j^k) \, b_j^k$$

where $\theta_j^k \leq \eta_j^k < \infty$, and θ_j^k denotes the specified minimum. One specific form of this program that might go a long way toward reducing losses attributable to misallocation of installed capital goods would be the form of (2.36) but with θ_j^k set equal $(1 - d_j^k)$. Reductions in economic activity would then be limited to the rate of depreciation of installed capital stock. That is, installed capital would be eliminated only at its natural rate of depreciation.

One such constraint for each industry in each region could be expressed as the following set of constraints for the interregional optimization program (2.24):

$$(2.37) \qquad \sum_j x_j^k \geq \left(\eta_j^k + d_j^k\right) b_j^k$$

where (2.33) corresponds to the case of $\eta_j^k = 1$ and, in general,

$$0 \leq \eta_j^k < \infty,$$

$$0 \leq d_j^k < 1, \text{ and}$$

$$0 \leq b_j^k \leq 1.$$

Note that such constraints would be regionally independent. They would not, therefore, alter the conclusions relating to the equality of regionally and supraregionally optimal portfolios.

Relaxation of the assumption that every industry in the feasibility set is infinitely divisible requires departing from the comfortable world of continuous feasibility space and entering the world of discrete feasibility sets. The universe of potential industrial structures is reduced from one that contained multiply infinite potential structures to a finite set of potential structures. The efficiency frontier of the feasibility set will no longer be continuous, as in Figure 2.1. Rather, it will consist of a set of discrete points corresponding to the expected returns and portfolio variances of the discrete set of possible industrial structures. The efficiency frontier in Figure 2.3 is one of this type.

Let us specify that each of J different industries is capable of producing at M_j discrete scales ($m_j = 1, 2, \ldots, M_j$). In order to allow for the possibility of more than one plant of each scale, let us further specify that the total relevant multiregional market would be satisfied by a total of N_j plants of a given scale in a given region ($n_j = 0, 1, 2, , , , , N_j$). Let the subscript $j_{n_j m_j}$ denote n plants of scale m in industry j, abbreviated j_{nm}.[7]

The total number of distinct plant and scale combinations for each industry is, therefore, $n_j m_j$. Given J different industries, the total number of elements in the universe of industries, plants and scales from which portfolios may be formed is:

$$(2.38) \qquad Q = J \sum_{j=1}^{J} n_j m_j.$$

The total number of distinct (unordered) potential portfolios from among which to select an optimum is:

$$(2.39) \qquad \sum_{r=1}^{J} \left(J \sum_{j} n_j m_j \atop r \right) = \sum_{r=1}^{J} \binom{Q}{r} = \sum_{r=1}^{J} \left(\frac{Q!}{r!(Q-r)!} \right).$$

To each of these portfolios there will correspond a vector of $x_j^k{}_{nm}$, the average share of total resources of each region required for each industry in the portfolio at the scale and number of plants at which each is included. Feasible portfolios for each region will consist of those for which $\sum_j \sum_n \sum_m x_{jnm} \leq 1$. Note that under this specification the separation theorem no longer holds, for the indivisibilities that have been introduced mean that some industrial assets will not be feasible components of some regional portfolios since in their smallest scales they would require more than the total available resources. The lack of the separation theorem, however, will not significantly alter the nature of the programming problem in this case. And the feasibility constraint

---

7. For example, $\mu_3{}^6 24$ denotes the expected return to region 6 of 2 plants of scale 4 with industry 3. The cumbersome notation appears to be valuable for preserving the continuity of approach and for making subsequent analyses readily comparable to those that have preceded.

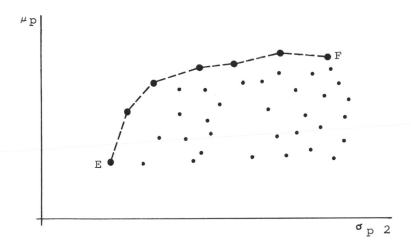

FIGURE 2.3

Mean-Variance Space and the Efficiency Frontier
(discrete feasible set because of indivisibility)

as given will effectively eliminate from the portfolio any industries whose minimum scale is too large for that region's resources.

The programming problem for determining the single optimum from among the feasibility set may be set up in binary form. Let $x^k_{j\,nm}$ be considered a parameter associated with the element identified by j_{nm} in k and let $C^k_{j\,nm}$ be a binary variable (taking only the value of zero or one). Then, the maximum problem becomes:

$$(2.40) \quad \operatorname*{Max}_{C} f(U) = \sum_k^K \sum_j^J \sum_{n_j}^{N_j} \sum_{m_j}^{M_j} \hat{x}^k_{j\,nm}\,\mu^k_{j\,nm}\,C^k_{j\,nm}$$

$$-\gamma \sum_k^K \sum_i^J \sum_j^J \sum_{n_{i,j}}^{N_{i,j}} \sum_{m_{i,j}}^{M_{i,j}} \hat{x}^k_{j\,nm}\,C^k_{j\,nm}\,\hat{x}^j_{i\,nm}\,C^j_{i\,nm}\,\sigma_{ij}$$

subject to the basic portfolio feasibility constraints,

$$(2.40a) \quad \sum_j \sum_n \sum_m \hat{x}^k_{j\,nm} \le 1, \text{ for all } k;$$

41

the preexisting industries constraint set,

$$(2.40b) \qquad \sum_{j=1}^{g} \sum_{n} \sum_{m} x_{j\,nm}^{k} \geq (n_{j\,nm}^{k} + d_{j\,nm}^{k}) \, b_{j}^{k}, \text{ for all } k;$$

the binary variable constraint set,

$$(2.40c) \qquad C_{j\,nm}^{k} = 0, \, 1 \text{ for all } k, \, j, \, n, \, m;$$

and the basic nonnegativity constraints,

$$(2.40d) \qquad \hat{x}_{j\,nm}^{k} \geq 0 \text{ for all } k, \, j, \, n, \, m.$$

This nonlinear binary stochastic programming problem may be solved by using either the Land-Doig branch and bound method [25], the Gomory cutting plane method [17], or the additional techniques suggested by McMillan [35, pp. 334-62].

In this format, furthermore, a number of additional relevant elements may be introduced. The value of $\mu_{j}^{k}\mathrm{nm}$ within a given region may or may not vary proportionally over different numbers of plants (that is, different size agglomerations). If, for example, there were no economies of scale internal to the firm to be reaped in a given industry, we would have

$$(2.41) \qquad \mu_{j\,n1}^{k} = \mu_{j\,n2}^{k} = \cdots = \mu_{j\,nM}^{k}$$

where scale 1 is considered smaller than scale 2, etc. If, on the other hand, such internalizable economies of scale were available, we would have to incorporate into the program

$$(2.42) \qquad \mu_{j\,n1}^{k} \leq \mu_{j\,n2}^{k} \leq \cdots \leq \mu_{j\,nM}^{k}.$$

Similarly, for any combination of increasing and decreasing returns to scale internal to the firm, the appropriate variation in specified returns may be introduced.

If there existed economies of scale external to the firm but internal to the industry (economies of specialization or agglomeration), then one could specify, for example,

$$(2.43) \qquad \mu_{j\,1m}^{k} \leq \mu_{j\,2m}^{k} \leq \mu_{j\,Nm}^{k}.$$

Diseconomies of scale would also be implementable by means of reversing the appropriate inequalities at the point at which they set in.

The more general and more ephemeral form of external economies, those external to both firm and industry, could be introduced, furthermore, by establishing higher values of $\mu_{j}^{k}\mathrm{nm}$ for regions with larger total stocks of resources.

THE PORTFOLIO VARIANCE AS A THEORETICAL MEASURE
OF RELATIVE DIVERSIFICATION

The pursuit of diversification without restraint is seldom likely to be a rational policy. Only in the operationally implausible context of identical returns from all efficient portfolios (a linear efficiency frontier perpendicular to the expected returns axis) will one diversify optimally by minimizing risk absolutely. The portfolio variance will, nevertheless, theoretically establish a unique rank-ordering of all portfolios with a given expected return according to the relative magnitude of the risk in each (as measured by the variance). If that risk is a measure of instability or fluctuation in return, the portfolio variance for portfolios with any given expected level of return will fall directly with the introduction of diversifying elements.

If we assume, for example, that all regions face the same universe of industries from which to choose and that all industries possess the same covariances in all regions (though their expected returns may vary), then that region which has the smallest portfolio variance has combined different industries in a maximally diversifying manner. It has reduced its theoretical fluctuations to the relatively smallest amount. That diversification may not be optimal for all regions, but it is the greatest given the feasibility set.

In Chapter 1 we suggested that an ideal measure of diversification would possess certain attributes. It would (1) reflect only the appropriate "differences" among the elements to be combined, here industries; (2) indicate greater diversification through addition of a new element only to the extent that the new element was appropriately different; (3) be sensitive to changes in the distribution of elements in the direction of greater "differences"; and (4) be independent of other structural characteristics. The portfolio variance seems to fill all the requirements.

The portfolio variance is the weighted sum of all portfolio covariances, as shown below in equation (2.45). It multiplies the proportion of total resources employed in an industry times that industry's theoretical contribution to aggregate instability, that is, its variance plus the sum of its covariances with other existing industries, all appropriately weighted. The appropriate differences for diversification of the portfolio are precisely these individual contributions to the aggregate measure of instability. The addition of a new industry is measured by the addition of its variance to the sum of variances and the addition of the sum of its covariance to the portfolio covariance. So long as it has sufficiently negative covariances with either many or large existing industries it can actually reduce the aggregate or total portfolio variance. Changes in the distribution of industries are effected in the same way and effect the portfolio variance similarly. If the increase in individual variance times the increase in the weight being given to an existing industry is less than the weight times the increase in (negative) covariance, total portfolio variance will be reduced. And the portfolio variance, if well estimated, need reflect no other structural characteristics. High portfolio variances may come from heavy weights upon individually highly variable industries or upon industries with high positive covariability, both of which are to be avoided in the interest of lower aggregate instability.

The relationship between SIC-based industry groups and the portfolio variance provides a clear example of the difference between it and the other measures of diversification. The ogive measure discussed in Chapter 1, for example, sums across SIC groups while weighting them only by the relative size as measured by squared deviations from ideal weights.

$$(2.44) \qquad \text{Ogive measure: } Q = \sum_{j}^{J} \frac{(w_j - w^*)^2}{w^*}$$

where w_j = relative weight of industry j, and
w^* = ideal weight = $1/J$.

The portfolio variance, as a measure of industrial diversification, sums across SIC groups while weighting each by its relative size times the precise relevant difference between each group and all others, their variances and covariances.

Portfolio variances measure:

$$(2.45) \qquad \sigma_p^{\,2} = \sum_{j}^{J} \sum_{i}^{J} w_j w_i \sigma_{ij}$$

where w_j denotes the relative weight of industry j, and
w_i denotes the relative weight of each industry i also in the region.

Given the variance as the appropriate measure of the fluctuations in returns, then not only is the portfolio variance an ideal measure of diversification, it is the ideal measure of diversification. This is not to say that no other ideal measure of industrial diversification may exist. For each alternative measure of fluctuation (for example, the semivariance), there will exist a comparably appropriate measure of diversification. This class of ideal measures of diversification is related to the class of alternative forms of measuring the risk against which one is diversifying and the set of alternative measures of that risk.

It is in this context that the theoretical capability of regions to diversify to a level of fluctuations far less than that of the nation and, consequently, to reduce national levels of fluctuation becomes apparent. National fluctuations in industrial activities consist, statistically, of weighted sums of the respective regional fluctuations. The theoretical national portfolio variance can be shown to consist of the weighted sum of regional portfolio variances. And any reduction, through diversification, of the regional portfolio variances may be expected to reduce national fluctuations.

Let $(\sigma_p^2)^N$ be the national industrial portfolio variance, and let w_j^N denote the relative magnitude of industry j in the nation as a whole (measured according to whatever form of fluctuations are being considered). Then

$$(2.46) \qquad (\sigma_p^2)^N = \sum_i \sum_j w_i^N w_j^N \sigma_{ij}.$$

Now the relative national magnitude of an industry is nothing more than the sum of relative regional magnitudes, $w_j^N = \sum_k w_j^k$. If $\sigma_{ij}^k = \sigma_{ij}^\ell$ for all ℓ and k (k, ℓ = 1, 2, . . . , K), then for K regions,

$$(2.47) \qquad (\sigma_p^2)^N = \sum_i \sum_j w_i^N w_j^N \sigma_{ij}$$

$$= \sum_i \sum_j \sum_k w_i^k w_j^k \sigma_{ij}, \quad \text{since } w_j^N = \sum_k w_j^k;$$

$$= \sum_k \sum_i \sum_j w_i^k w_j^k \sigma_{ij}$$

$$= \sum_k (\sigma_p^2)^k.$$

The significance of this conclusion rests with the potential national impact of individual regions diversifying their respective industrial structures so as to reduce their theoretical levels of fluctuation as measured by their respective portfolio variances. We have seen that any region can obtain theoretical stability greater than that of the nation as a whole by distributing its resources among a less variable subset of industries than those that characterize the nation as a whole. We have seen that, under open interregional trade and identical aversion to risk, individual regionally optimal diversification is consistent with nationally optimal diversification. And we see now that successful diversification of individual regions (successful in the sense of reducing regional portfolio variances) will lead to a theoretical reduction in national instability.

3

INDUSTRIAL
DIVERSIFICATION
AND RELATIVE
INSTABILITY IN U.S.
METROPOLITAN REGIONS

In Chapter 2 we considered in some detail the derivation of an optimally diversified portfolio of industries for a region. We also suggested that the portfolio variance offers a theoretically improved index of relative diversification in that it fulfills the prerequisites for an ideal measure established in Chapter 1. We had noted there the skepticism that surrounds the analysis of the "industrial structure" variable, and we noted some of the conceptual and practical difficulties that have hindered analysis of the relationship between industrial structure and relative regional fluctuations.

In this chapter we report the results of a limited analysis of the relationship between fluctuations in economic activity and the nature of the industrial structure for a set of U.S. regions. The analysis was focused on three questions:

1. To what extent have the fluctuations in economic activity of the U.S. regions been related to the relative diversification of their respective industrial structures?

2. Does the portfolio variance of those industrial structures offer a better predictor of the instability of an industrial structure than the alternative measures discussed in Chapter 1, such as the relative magnitude of durable goods production, deviation from a rectangular distribution across all industries, or deviation from the national average for each industry across all regions?

3. To what extent and in what direction has the instability of economic activity been influenced by general characteristics of the region such as absolute size, rate of growth, and general location within the country?

In brief, the empirical procedure underlying the results presented here consisted of the following. Indices of instability of aggregate manufacturing employment were calculated for 52 Standard Metropolitan Statistical Areas for the 120 months from January 1958 through December 1967. Estimates of the distribution of manufacturing employment among

118 essentially 3-digit SIC categories were made for each of the regions. The variance-covariance matrix for employment in the 118 industry groups was estimated from time series for each industry at the national level for the same time period. The portfolio variance for each region was then calculated using the common variance-covariance matrix. For purposes of strict comparability, the alternative measures were also calculated from the same set of employment estimates for each region on the basis of 118 industries. Simple and multivariate statistical analysis was then used to determine the nature, magnitude, and significance of the relationships suggested by the data.

This empirical analysis may be shown to relate to the preceding theoretical discussion by assuming that the sole "return" to the region with respect to which diversification is sought is the level of manufacturing employment around a given level of employment. Conversely, they may be viewed as efforts that seek to maximize the level of manufacturing employment associated with a given level of fluctuations or instability.

Such analysis in terms of employment levels alone is subject to a number of well-known criticisms [for example, Nourse, 40, pp. 161-62]. For one thing, incomes vary among occupations; regions cannot easily be assumed to be indifferent to such differences. More important here, use of employment alone as a measure of return implies that larger cities are necessarily to be preferred to smaller cities. This is, of course, not necessarily true. Nonetheless, despite the recent upsurge in questioning of growth (and particularly unplanned growth), there are few areas or regions today that have articulated or that are attempting to implement policies of zero economic growth or zero employment growth. Some growth remains an objective.

Use of manufacturing employment as a measure of desired "return" from regional investment of real factor assets in alternative manufacturing activities, therefore, is intended to provide a conceptually and statistically simplified demonstration of the analysis of industrial diversification that admittedly omits many dimensions of the problem. There is no implication intended here that larger metropolitan areas are necessarily preferable; but there is an implication that increases in employment levels and reductions in levels of fluctuations in employment are generally to be accepted as valid goals of regional planners at specific points in time and space.

THE REGIONAL EMPLOYMENT DATA

The basic data from which the index of instability for each region was constructed consist of monthly aggregate manufacturing employment for each of 52 Standard Metropolitan Statistical Areas. The data represent the latest revised estimates reported to the Bureau of Labor Statistics (BLS) by cooperating state employment security agencies or state

47

departments of labor and published in the monthly Employment and Earnings series [67]. They cover the period from January 1958 through December 1967, a total of 120 months.

The choice of time span and the sample of regions to include was dictated almost entirely by the availablility of data. Three constraints on availability were binding. First, the Standard Industrial Classification Manual [70] was revised in 1957 and 1967 and supplemented in 1963. The revisions of 1957 and 1967 were so extensive that unless substantial revision of data is undertaken at even the 1-digit level, no consistent time series is available for many industries and many regions. The Employment and Earnings statistics were reported on a consistent 1957 SIC basis from January 1958 through December 1967. Prior to that they were reported on a 1945 SIC basis, and subsequently they have been reported on the 1967 basis. The 1957 revisions included the transfer of a number of industries and industry groups from trade to manufacturing and an even larger number of industries (4-digit level) to new industry groups (3-digit level) [70, p. 15]. The 1963 Supplement to the 1957 code contained changes that were limited to reclassification of activities among 4-digit industries, always within preexisting 3-digit groups. Time series sensitive to SIC changes at the 3-digit or higher levels were, therefore, unaffected by the Supplement [72, p. 9].

The second constraint on time span and areal coverage was a function of the constant process of redefinition that the geographic boundaries of SMSAs have undergone. This process limited the usable SMSAs to those that were defined in 1958 and that underwent no change in boundaries or those for which revised manufacturing employment data, consistent with the December 1967 geographic boundaries had been prepared by the various state agencies. The 52 SMSAs ultimately included in the study represent the largest number for which manufacturing employment data could be obtained on a geographically consistent basis either from the cooperating state agencies or from the Employment and Earnings series directly. Approximately 80 percent of the data in the resulting 52 120-month time series came from the state agencies. The remainder was taken from individual issues of the published series at the latest date at which each was available (generally 15 months after the reported month) in order to incorporate the latest revisions. All the time series thus obtained consist of raw data, unadjusted for seasonality. [1]

In the process of requesting data from the cooperating state agencies, it was discovered that for numerous SMSAs, 49 of the 52, data from 1956, 1955, and earlier years had been revised to the 1957 SIC code. It was at this point, however, that the third constraint on the length of the time series became binding. In order to estimate the

1. For details on the standardized sampling and estimating procedures used by the agencies to obtain their estimates, see the "Technical Note" published at the back of each issue of Employment and Earnings.

variance-covariance matrix among industries for a period comparable to that from which the indices of instability were to be calculated, it was necessary to obtain disaggregated time series on individual industries at the national level. These series are available in the BLS bulletin Employment and Earnings, United States, 1909-68 [68]. The revisions of the SIC code of 1957 were so extensive that nearly half the monthly series presented there at the 3-digit level are unavailable prior to January 1958. Hence, the time span used.

The set of metropolitan regions consequently included is given in Table 3.1, along with several items of descriptive data associated with each. The counties of which each SMSA was composed as of the May 1967 definition may be found in Appendix Table A.3.1. The 1963 level of manufacturing employment is the arithmetic mean of the monthly data for that year from the time series discussed above. The rates of growth of manufacturing employment are geometric mean rates of annual change based upon arithmetic averages of the raw data for each year. The population figures are 1960 Census figures taken from the County and City Book, 1967 as adjusted there to correspond to the 1967 geographic definitions [65].

The sample set of SMSAs includes a total 1960 population of 60.4 million, 51.6 percent of total U.S. population in SMSAs, and total manufacturing employment of 6.7 million, 39.5 percent of total U.S. manufacturing employment for the reference year. It includes cities from all 9 major census regions and from 27 different states.[2] The metropolitan area populations of the cities range from 73,000 to 10 million, and the manufacturing employment ranges from 4,200 to slightly over 1 million. Few of the cities would be considered "small" by most criteria; only 7 had a total population under 250,000 in 1960. Fourteen of the 52 had metropolitan area populations above 1 million, and the mean population for the group was nearly 1.2 million. Yet 26 of the 52 had 1960 population under 500,000 and would not, therefore, be considered "very large" cities by twentieth-century standards.

INDICES OF INSTABILITY

For each of the 52 regions thus defined three indices of instability were calculated: one based on raw data, one based on detrended data, and one based on data from which both trend and seasonality had been removed. The basic form of all the indices calculated is the coefficient of variation, a measure of relative dispersion that is defined in its simplest (sample) form as

---

2. Hereafter the terms "city," "region," and "SMSA" will be used synonymously, unless otherwise indicated, to refer to the SMSAs in the sample.

TABLE 3.1

The Sample of Regions:
52 SMSAs with Summary Statistics

Metropolitan Region	1960 Population (000s)	1963 Manufacturing Employment (000s)	Annual Growth Rate, Manufacturing Employment (1958-67)
1 Albany	657. 5	61. 8	-0. 00791 (50)
2 Albuquerque	262. 2	8. 5	0. 01848 (28)
3 Allentown et al.	492. 2	93. 6	0. 01129 (34)
4 Atlanta	1, 017. 2	96. 3	0. 03923 (6)
5 Baltimore	1, 727. 0	194. 4	0. 00593 (41)
6 Baton Rouge	230. 1	15. 8	-0. 00888 (51)
7 Binghamton	283. 6	42. 7	-0. 00030 (46)
8 Buffalo	1, 307. 0	164. 9	0. 00168 (44)
9 Chattanooga	283. 2	39. 7	0. 02442 (20)
10 Chicago	6, 220. 9	849. 0	0. 01646 (30)
11 Dallas	1, 083. 6	111. 0	0. 04748 (4)
12 Denver	929. 4	68. 9	0. 03777 (7)
13 Detroit	3, 762. 3	501. 3	0. 02194 (24)
14 Erie	250. 7	36. 9	0. 02162 (26)
15 Fort Wayne	232. 2	36. 5	0. 03416 (12)
16 Fresno	365. 9	14. 9	0. 02498 (19)
17 Gary et al.	573. 5	98. 9	0. 00658 (40)
18 Great Falls	73. 4	4. 2	0. 00920 (37)
19 Greensboro et al.	246. 5	44. 5	0. 02184 (25)
20 Indianapolis	916. 9	115. 8	0. 02639 (17)
21 Knoxville	368. 0	42. 4	0. 01958 (27)
22 Lancaster	278. 4	47. 9	0. 02333 (22)
23 Los Angeles et al.	6, 038. 7	754. 3	0. 02283 (22)
24 Miami	935. 0	46. 4	0. 05459 (3)
25 Minneapolis et al.	1, 482. 0	160. 2	0. 03658 (8)

	Metropolitan Region	1960 Population (000s)	1963 Manufacturing Employment (000s)	Annual Growth Rate, Manufacturing Employment (1958-67)
26	New York	10,695.0	1096.6	-0.00399 (48)
27	Omaha et al.	457.9	35.1	0.01559 (31)
28	Philadelphia	4,342.9	536.2	0.00972 (36)
29	Phoenix	663.5	41.1	0.09339 (1)
30	Pittsburgh	2,405.4	268.2	-0.00267 (47)
31	Portland	821.9	66.8	0.03540 (10)
32	Racine	141.8	22.2	0.02774 (16)
33	Reading	275.4	51.6	0.01737 (29)
34	Rochester	732.6	121.5	0.02604 (18)
35	Salt Lake City	447.8	32.0	0.03520 (11)
36	San Diego	1,033.0	56.5	-0.01257 (52)
37	San Francisco et al.	2,648.8	195.0	0.00860 (38)
38	San Jose	642.3	86.8	0.08906 (2)
39	Savannah	188.3	14.3	0.01035 (35)
40	Seattle et al.	1,107.2	120.1	0.03525 (9)
41	Sioux Falls	86.6	5.4	0.00688 (39)
42	Spokane	278.3	12.3	-0.00676 (49)
43	Stockton	250.0	13.1	0.02970 (15)
44	Syracuse	563.8	63.9	0.00211 (43)
45	Tacoma	321.6	16.8	0.02415 (21)
46	Tampa et al.	772.5	37.9	0.04066 (5)
47	Topeka	141.3	6.8	0.03055 (14)
48	Trenton	266.4	38.2	0.01250 (33)
49	Tucson	265.7	9.3	-0.00021 (45)
50	Utica et al.	330.8	38.0	0.00587 (42)
51	Wilkes Barre et al.	347.0	44.1	0.03332 (13)
52	Winston-Salem	189.4	37.2	0.01274 (32)
	Mean	1,162.2	129.2	0.02089
	Standard Deviation	1,905.1	221.6	0.02095

Source: Population Figures from County and City Data Book, 1967 (Washington, D.C.: Government Printing Office, 1967); manufacturing employment and rates of growth calculated by the author from monthly issues of Employment and Earnings (Washington, D.C.: Government Printing Office, 1958-67).

$$(3.1) \qquad Z_c^{Ik} = \left[\frac{\sum\limits_{t=1}^{N}\left(\dfrac{y_t^k - \bar{y}^k}{\bar{y}^k}\right)^2}{N-1}\right]^{\frac{1}{2}}$$

where Z_c^{Ik} denotes the sample coefficient of variation calculated from unadjusted data (data series I) for region k;

y_t^k denotes individual observations, $t = 1, 2, \ldots, N$; and

$\bar{y}^k$ denotes the arithmetic mean of the series of observations.

In this form the index suffers from one major fault. It will give a biased indication of instability for those regions with any growth trend, whether positive or negative; for the norm with respect to which deviations are measured is the mean of the observations over the entire period. As indicated in Figure 3.1, this is equivalent to measuring deviations from a horizontal line through the mean of the time series. Regions that have employment levels that fluctuate very little but that are growing steadily over time will be inappropriately classed as relatively unstable regions by this index. The fluctuations in employment that are, for most cases, the most relevant are those with respect to the specific trend. That is, for example, in the medium term the relatively unstable region is that region that fluctuates greatly around its longer-run trend, whatever that trend.

Regression techniques were used to eliminate the trend from each of the 52 employment time series. Equations of the following form were estimated for each of the series:

$$(3.2) \qquad y_t^k = \alpha^k + \beta_1^k t + \beta_2^k t^2 + \varepsilon$$

where t denotes the time vector ($t = 1, 2, \ldots, 120$) for region k,

ε denotes the random component assumed to be a random variable which is independently distributed with a mean of zero and a variance of 1, and

α, β_1, and β_2 denote the partial regression parameters to be estimated.

For each region, then, the estimated equations were used to predict $\hat{y}_t^k$ where

$$(3.3) \qquad \hat{y}_t^k = \bar{\alpha}^k + \bar{\beta}_1^k t + \bar{\beta}_2^k t^2$$

and where $\bar{\alpha}^k$, $\bar{\beta}_1^k$, and $\bar{\beta}_2^k$ denotes the previously estimated parameters of the trend equation for region k.

Finally, a coefficient of variation of the residuals around such a trend was calculated for each region. We shall denote it Z_c^{II}.

FIGURE 3.1

Comparative Bases for Measurement
of Fluctuation over Time
(hypothetical highly seasonal data)

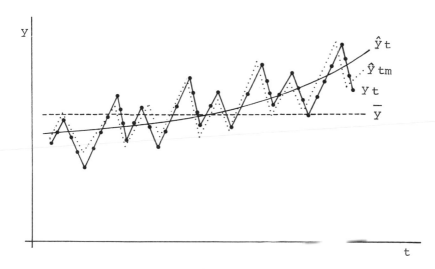

where

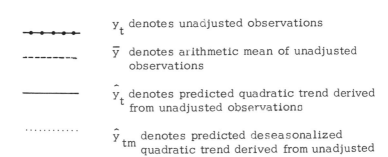

y_t denotes unadjusted observations

$\bar{y}$ denotes arithmetic mean of unadjusted
observations

$\hat{y}_t$ denotes predicted quadratic trend derived
from unadjusted observations

$\hat{y}_{tm}$ denotes predicted deseasonalized
quadratic trend derived from unadjusted
observations

$$(3.4) \qquad Z_c^{\;\; \Pi^k} = \left[\frac{\sum\limits_{t=1}^{N} \left(\dfrac{y_t^k - \hat{y}_t^k}{\bar{y}^k} \right)^2}{N-2} \right]^{-\frac{1}{2}}$$

The functional form for the trend was chosen on the basis of three criteria. First, a random sample of 30 regions and industry groups (for use in subsequent estimation of covariance matrices) was regressed against three alternative time trends: linear, quadratic, and exponential (log linear). Employing the techniques suggested by Goldberger [15, pp. 125-34] and considering all 30 sets of regressions as a whole, the sum of the error sum of squares was minimized and the mean of the coefficients of determination (adjusted for degrees of freedom) was minimized by the quadratic form. Second, the quadratic form also fit the aggregate U.S. manufacturing employment series for the same time span better than either alternative. Third, the quadratic form includes, as a subset of its own form, the linear form that was next best fitting. For when β_2^k in equation (3.2) is equal to zero, equation (3.2) becomes linear.

The treatment of seasonality in time series such as those considered here raises a number of conceptual questions. The two most recent quantitative studies of relative regional fluctuations, those of Siegel [53] and Cutler and Hansz [10], used deseasonalized series without comment. The use of such deseasonalized series implies that seasonal variation is of no concern to the policy maker. Thompson [19] has noted that stable, predictable seasonal variation leads to underutilization of resources. Increases in efficiency can be accomplished by spreading the demand for such resources over longer periods of time or by finding complementary uses for them. In general, one may suggest, seasonal variation should be of no concern to economic policy makers only in that situation where seasonal resource flows (such as migrant labor) increase capacity at the point in space and time when peak seasonal demand occurs and where such resource flows have relatively low opportunity costs. Any seasonality not inducing the needed temporary resource flows is a source of inefficiency and, therefore, is a proper object of stabilization policy.

The magnitude of such resource flows in the United States, though substantial within some industries such as food processing, are unlikely to be of sufficient magnitude and are unlikely to be of sufficiently low cost to warrant the ignoring of seasonal fluctuations that is inherent in working only with deseasonalized data. For that reason the detrended but not deseasonalized series, series II, will be treated most extensively in the discussion that follows. It is the series that we consider most important in that it is the series most likely to be relevant to most policy makers.

For purposes of completeness and comparability, however, an index of instability was also calculated for each region from detrended and deseasonalized data. The procedure was similar to that for detrending alone. Following the caveats of Lovell [30] and Nerlove [38] about traditional forms of deseasonalizing, and making use of the alternative technique suggested by Lovell, equations of the following form were estimated for each of the regions:

$$(3.5) \qquad y_{tm}^k = \alpha^k + \beta_1^k t + \beta_2^k t^2 + \sum_{i=3}^{14} \beta_i^k S_{tmi} + \varepsilon_{tm}$$

where $S_{tmi} = \begin{cases} 1 \text{ if } i - 2 = m \text{ and} \\ 0 \text{ otherwise,} \end{cases}$

    m denotes the number of the month to which each observation corresponds, $m = 1, 2, \ldots, 11.$ [3]
For each region the estimated equations were used to predict $\hat{y}_{tm}^k$, where, as before,

$$(3.6) \qquad \hat{y}_{tm}^k = \hat{\alpha}^k + \bar{\beta}_1^k t + \bar{\beta}_2^k t^2 + \sum_{i=3}^{14} \bar{\beta}_i^k S_{tmi}.$$

Finally, a coefficient of variation of the residuals around such a trend was calculated and named Z_c^{III}, where

$$(3.7) \qquad Z_c^{III^k} = \left[\sum_{t=1}^{N} \left(\frac{y_t^k - \hat{y}_{tm}^k}{\bar{y}^k} \right)^2 \Bigg/ N - 13 \right]^{\frac{1}{2}}$$

The resulting three indices of instability for each region are listed in Table 3.2. The respective $\bar{y}^k$ that will permit transformation of these measures of relative fluctuation into comparable measures of absolute fluctuations that are not independent of city size, but that may be useful, are reproduced in Appendix Table A.3.4.

The values listed in Table 3.2 may be interpreted, perhaps most clearly, as the standard deviation of fluctuations in SMSA manufacturing employment expressed as a percentage of the mean employment level for that SMSA for the period under consideration. Thus, for the detrended series (hereafter referred to as "the main series"), Great Falls, Montana,

---

3. Since it would be clearly unrealistic to eliminate the constant term, α^k, and to imply thereby that employment levels were zero at time 0, the dummy block created for equation (3.5) was only 120 x 11, a technique suggested by Wonnacott and Wonnacott [78], among others, to avoid singularity. The seasonality of the twelfth month, if any, was captured by the constant term.

TABLE 3.2

Empirical Indices of Relative Instability:
Coefficients of Variation of Alternative Data Sets
(column ranks in parentheses)

Metropolitan Region	Z_c^{I} (Unadjusted)	Z_c^{II} (Detrended)	Z_c^{III} (Detrended and Deseasonalized)
1 Albany	.04850 (41)	.03042 (36)	.03074 (34)
2 Albuquerque	.07509 (29)	.04084 (21)	.04037 (16)
3 Allentown et al.	.05264 (37)	.03076 (35)	.03135 (32)
4 Atlanta	.13523 (9)	.03660 (25)	.03757 (19)
5 Baltimore	.03378 (50)	.02335 (48)	.02368 (44)
6 Baton Rouge	.08525 (25)	.05846 (10)	.05856 (6)
7 Binghamton	.04001 (47)	.03028 (38)	.03131 (33)
8 Buffalo	.04286 (44)	.03208 (31)	.03198 (31)
9 Chattanooga	.09533 (21)	.03665 (24)	.03784 (18)
10 Chicago	.05865 (36)	.02400 (47)	.02466 (40)
11 Dallas	.15934 (6)	.01758 (52)	.01737 (49)
12 Denver	.09732 (20)	.05766 (11)	.05850 (7)
13 Detroit	.09924 (19)	.06063 (9)	.05705 (8)
14 Erie	.08913 (23)	.03638 (26)	.03497 (24)
15 Fort Wayne	.10878 (17)	.04167 (20)	.04193 (15)
16 Fresno	.12128 (12)	.09822 (4)	.02654 (38)
17 Gary et al.	.08374 (26)	.07946 (7)	.07903 (5)
18 Great Falls	.21865 (3)	.19348 (1)	.20038 (1)
19 Greensboro et al.	.06690 (31)	.01870 (51)	.01915 (48)
20 Indianapolis	.08335 (27)	.03140 (33)	.03281 (29)
21 Knoxville	.06376 (34)	.02306 (49)	.02327 (45)
22 Lancaster	.07328 (30)	.02451 (46)	.02413 (42)
23 Los Angeles et al.	.06297 (35)	.02880 (39)	.02963 (36)
24 Miami	.16386 (5)	.03197 (32)	.02243 (46)
25 Minneapolis et al.	.11317 (16)	.02490 (44)	.02401 (43)

	Metropolitan Region	Z_c^{I} (Unadjusted)	Z_c^{II} (Detrended)	Z_c^{III} (Detrended and Deseasonalized)
26	New York	.03052 (52)	.02464 (45)	.01612 (51)
27	Omaha et al.	.04184 (45)	.03594 (27)	.03723 (20)
28	Philadelphia	.03063 (51)	.01958 (50)	.02031 (47)
29	Phoenix	.27881 (1)	.05005 (13)	.05186 (11)
30	Pittsburgh	.06543 (32)	.05650 (12)	.05598 (9)
31	Portland	.11537 (15)	.04716 (15)	.03224 (30)
32	Racine	.11611 (14)	.04579 (17)	.04660 (13)
33	Reading	.05068 (39)	.02506 (43)	.02442 (41)
34	Rochester	.08829 (24)	.02474 (42)	.01515 (52)
35	Salt Lake City	.12535 (11)	.04250 (19)	.04333 (14)
36	San Diego	.12691 (10)	.08244 (5)	.08567 (3)
37	San Francisco et al.	.03656 (49)	.03033 (37)	.01669 (50)
38	San Jose	.24298 (2)	.06946 (8)	.05417 (10)
39	Savannah	.04814 (42)	.03259 (30)	.03288 (28)
40	Seattle et al.	.14401 (7)	.08062 (6)	.08257 (4)
41	Sioux Falls	.04096 (46)	.03774 (23)	.03379 (27)
42	Spokane	.05245 (38)	.04798 (14)	.03714 (21)
43	Stockton	.19497 (4)	.17113 (2)	.04872 (12)
44	Syracuse	.03727 (48)	.03367 (29)	.03407 (25)
45	Tacoma	.08264 (28)	.04657 (16)	.03680 (22)
46	Tampa et al.	.11750 (13)	.02827 (41)	.02587 (39)
47	Topeka	.09099 (22)	.03093 (34)	.02977 (35)
48	Trenton	.06378 (33)	.03940 (22)	.03955 (17)
49	Tucson	.13583 (8)	.12280 (3)	.12876 (2)
50	Utica et al.	.05019 (40)	.03498 (28)	.03526 (23)
51	Wilkes-Barre et al.	.10422 (18)	.02846 (40)	.02670 (37)
52	Winston-Salem	.04727 (43)	.04447 (18)	.03407 (25)
	Mean	.09292	.04705	.04163
	Standard Deviation	.19052	.03444	.03033

Source: Calculated by the author from BLS employment time series.

and Stockton, California, demonstrated the greatest instability of the 52 regions with Z_c^{II} equal to 19.3 and 17.1 percent of the ten-year mean employment level, respectively. For Stockton, however, unlike Great Falls, a very large part of that fluctuation is seasonal. This may be inferred from the fact that for Stockton, Z_c^{III}, the measure based on detrended and deseasonalized data, showed fluctuations of only 4.9 percent while Z_c^{III} corresponding to Great Falls was 20.0 percent. [4]

The theoretical bias against growth inherent in Z_c^{I} is also substantiated in the data of Table 3.2. Cities such as Atlanta, Dallas, Fort Wayne, San Jose, and Tampa, which were shown in Table 3.1 to have relatively high growth rates, are found in Table 3.2 with relatively very high apparent relative instability when such is measured by Z_c^{I} but much lower levels of instability when measured by Z_c^{II} or Z_c^{III}.

THE ESTIMATION OF REGIONAL INDUSTRIAL STRUCTURES

The first and perhaps foremost difficulty encountered in evaluating the significance of alternative industrial structures, where such are defined at a meaningfully disaggregated level, is the very determination of the relative structures for a set of regions. The "disclosure" policy of the Bureau of the Census makes that task a truly complicated one. The disclosure policy has created a situation in which the level of disaggregation possible for states or large cities is not possible for small cities, and one where industries for which data are provided at the 4-digit level for one city of a given size may not be listed completely at any level greater than 2-digits for another city of the same size.

There is thus created a trade-off between finer disaggregation (and consequently more meaningful levels of analysis) and the gaps that become apparent in the data due to disclosure problems (and consequently less-accurate analysis). In prior empirical analyses of relative regional fluctuations, no study known to this author has been able to proceed at levels of aggregation greater than 2-digit SIC.

One data source that makes it possible to avoid some of these problems is the special reports series entitled "The Location of Manufacturing Plants by County, Industry, and Employment Size" [66], which

---

4. The coefficients of variation of residuals from the detrended and deseasonalized series are marginally greater than those corresponding to the detrended series for a total of 27 of the regions. This apparent anomaly (larger residuals after the incusion of more variables) is a product of the fact that in those 27 regions the presence of seasonality was so slight that the increase in explanatory power of the greater number of variables was not sufficient to override the decrease in degrees of freedom occasioned by including more variables.

has been derived from the censuses of manufactures in 1957, 1963, and 1967. In this series the number of manufacturing plants in each county in the nation, disaggregated to the 4-digit SIC level, is distributed over six employment-size classes. The Census Bureau is willing to publish this data because, presumably, no exact figures are given for any plant in any county or industry. This inexactness is reinforced by the fact that the bureau will not disclose the means of the employment-size classes except those relating to all manufacturing in all counties. Table 3.3 presents the interval breakdown and the published means for this data.

Although no single-plant employment estimates could be derived with much confidence from this data, its usefulness for deriving aggregate estimates by industry of employment within multicounty regions is considerably greater. For the means of the size classes are in fact the maximum likelihood estimates of the number of employees in a plant in that class from a randomly selected county and industry. For any given county and industry the quality of the estimates could be improved substantially if regional means or disaggregated industry means were made available, but they were not. The possible crudeness of the estimates notwithstanding, the 1963 plant location data were used to generate estimates of the total employment in each of the 144 3-digit SIC groups within manufacturing for each of the 52 regions under study.

For each county that was a component of one of the 52 regions, the number of plants in each employment-size class in each 4-digit industry was identified, multiplied by the respective size-class mean, and summed to provide an estimate of total 1963 employment in that industry for that county. The resulting estimates were aggregated first across 4-digit SIC groups to the 3-digit level and then across component counties to the SMSA level as defined in Appendix Table A.3.1. Finally, for each SMSA the 3-digit employment estimates were summed to provide a derived estimate of total manufacturing employment, and the percentage distribution of employment among 3-digit industries was calculated on that basis.

The quality of the estimated employment totals for each industry in each region cannot, in general, be tested; the estimation process was necessary because the alternative data are generally unpublished. One set of tests of the quality of the estimates that was possible given published data was that based on total reported and total estimated employment by region. Table 3.4 presents the total manufacturing estimates and the reported data with which it was compared. Although percentage errors as great as 36.5 and -14.1 percent occur for individual regions, the overall quality may be considered fairly good and the estimates may be demonstrated to be unbiased. The Pearson correlation coefficient between the two sets of estimates is .9961. Given the rather large variation in city size, however, this correlation is not surprising.

Three simple hypothesis tests substantiate the lack of bias. First, testing whether the difference between the means of the two vectors of manufacturing employment is significantly different from zero, one

TABLE 3. 3

Standard Employment Size Classes
and Published 1963 Means for Each

Class (Employees)	Mean
1 - 19	6
20 - 49	31
50 - 99	69
100 - 249	155
250 - 499	346
500 - 999	684
1,000 +	2,545

Source: U.S. Census Bureau, "The Location of Manufacturing Plants by County, Industry, and Employment Size," 1963 Census of Manufactures, Special Reports (Washington, D.C.: Government Printing Office, 1966), p. iv.

cannot reject the null hypothesis (difference equal to zero) at a confidence level of .999. Similarly, tests of whether the mean of the vector of absolute errors or the mean of the vector of percentage errors (which eliminates the influence of relative size of the various regions) are significantly different from zero lead to the same conclusion. The null hypothesis cannot be rejected; the mean error is not significantly different from zero. [5]

The total manufacturing estimates for each region are also free of dependence upon the size of the region. None of the correlation coefficients between absolute or percentage error and total population or reported manufacturing were significantly different from zero at .05 level of significance.

---

5. Estimates by Latham [26] using the same technique for 199 selected 4-digit industries produced a correlation coefficient of .97. And estimates by him of 4-digit employment in each of the spatially all-inclusive 398 Office of Business Economics Personal Income regions produced, when summed across all regions, a vector of national industry employment estimates for 199 industries that had a correlation coefficient of .96 with reported employment in those industries.

TABLE 3.4

A Comparison of Reported Aggregate Employment in Manufacturing
and Estimates Based on the Plant Location Data

	Metropolitan Region	Reported 1963 Average	Estimated 1963 Average	Absolute Error	Percent Error
1	Albany	61.8	70.5	8.7	14.0
2	Albuquerque	8.5	8.0	-0.5	-5.8
3	Allentown et al.	93.6	82.8	-10.8	-11.5
4	Atlanta	96.3	94.6	-1.7	-1.7
5	Baltimore	194.4	174.5	-19.9	-10.2
6	Baton Rouge	15.8	13.6	-2.2	-13.9
7	Binghamton	42.7	34.8	-7.9	-18.5
8	Buffalo	164.9	161.2	-3.7	-2.2
9	Chattanooga	39.7	40.5	0.8	2.0
10	Chicago	849.0	885.5	36.5	4.2
11	Dallas	111.0	98.1	-12.9	-11.6
12	Denver	68.9	61.9	-7.0	-10.1
13	Detroit	501.3	451.6	-49.7	-9.9
14	Erie	36.8	40.5	3.7	10.0
15	Fort Wayne	36.5	39.5	3.0	8.2
16	Fresno	14.9	14.7	-0.2	-1.3
17	Gary et al.	98.9	67.8	-31.1	-31.4
18	Great Falls	4.2	2.7	-1.5	-35.7
19	Greensboro et al.	44.5	49.8	5.3	11.9
20	Indianapolis	115.8	104.6	-11.2	-9.6
21	Knoxville	42.4	35.6	-6.8	-16.0
22	Lancaster	47.9	52.8	4.9	10.2
23	Los Angeles et al.	754.3	670.6	-83.7	-11.0
24	Miami	46.4	46.0	-0.4	-0.8
25	Minneapolis et al.	160.2	164.9	4.7	2.9

(continued)

(Table 3.4 continued)

	Metropolitan Region	Reported 1963 Average	Estimated 1963 Average	Absolute Error	Percent Error
26	New York	1096.6	1164.5	67.9	6.1
27	Omaha et al.	35.1	37.2	2.1	5.9
28	Philadelphia	536.2	550.4	14.2	2.6
29	Phoenix	41.1	43.8	2.7	6.5
30	Pittsburgh	268.2	261.6	-6.6	-2.4
31	Portland	66.8	68.8	2.0	2.9
32	Racine	22.2	23.7	1.5	6.7
33	Reading	51.6	51.6	0.0	0.0
34	Rochester	121.5	99.7	-21.8	-17.9
35	Salt Lake City	32.0	29.0	-3.0	-9.3
36	San Diego	56.5	42.0	-14.5	-25.6
37	San Francisco et al.	195.0	215.0	20.0	10.2
38	San Jose	86.8	70.9	-15.9	-18.3
39	Savannah	14.3	15.9	1.6	11.1
40	Seattle et al.	120.1	76.3	-43.8	-36.4
41	Sioux Falls	5.4	5.3	-0.1	-1.8
42	Spokane	12.3	13.7	1.4	11.3
43	Stockton	13.1	14.6	1.5	11.4
44	Syracuse	63.9	65.5	1.6	2.5
45	Tacoma	16.8	17.1	0.3	1.7
46	Tampa et al.	37.9	37.6	-0.3	-0.7
47	Topeka	6.8	6.8	0.0	0.0
48	Trenton	38.2	41.9	3.7	9.6
49	Tucson	9.3	7.4	-1.9	-20.4
50	Utica et al.	38.0	42.7	4.7	12.3
51	Wilkes-Barre et al.	44.1	45.9	1.8	4.0
52	Winston-Salem	37.2	25.8	-11.4	-30.6
	Mean	129.1	125.8	10.87	.103
	Standard Deviation	221.6	225.1	17.21	.089
	Standard Error	30.7	31.2	2.39	.012

Source: Reported averages from Employment and Earnings (Washington, D.C.: Government Printing Office, 1958-67); estimated averages calculated by the author from census plant location data.

CALCULATION OF PORTFOLIO VARIANCES

The portfolio variance for each region, defined in equation (2.45), consists of the weighted sum of individual industry variances and covariances. In order to calculate the variance-covariance matrices for employment levels among alternative industries, reported monthly employment data for each industry within manufacturing were taken, as noted above, from the BLS series Employment and Earnings, United States, 1909-1968 [68]. The data presented there are not disaggregated to a complete 144 industry 3-digit SIC level. Rather, the data are organized into 117 modified groups that cover virtually all manufacturing at a 3-digit SIC level, except for Ordnance and armaments (SIC 19), which is covered completely only at the 2-digit level. The resulting 118 time series from January 1958 to December 1967 include 99.0 percent of all U.S. manufacturing employment as of 1963, the midpoint of the series. [6]

Three variance-covariance matrices were then calculated for the set of 118 industries, one based on raw data, one based on detrended data, and one based on detrended and deseasonalized data. In order to adjust for differences in the national magnitude of the respective industries and to provide interindustrially comparable statistics, the matrices consist of relative covariances rather than absolute covariances. Thus

---

6. The 118 industry groups are listed in Appendix Table A.3.2. The only 3-digit SIC groups omitted entirely from the published series (for unknown reasons) were the following:

Industry Group	Description	1963 Employment
SIC 213	Chewing and smoking tobacco	5,700
SIC 214	Tobacco stemming and drying	13,600
SIC 323	Products of purchased glass	18,900
	Total	38,200

Other than the inclusion of all Armaments and ordnance at the 2-digit level, the only differences from a strict 3-digit SIC coverage of all manufacturing are that 13 industry groups in the modified grouping contain from two to six 3-digit groups lumped together, always from within the same 2-digit major group. For example, the group that we identify as Group 261 and that we call "Paper and pulp mills" consist of SIC 261, "Pulp mills"; SIC 262, "Paper mills, except building paper mills"; and SIC 266, "Building paper and building board mills."

63

the matrix calculated from unadjusted data, denoted Σ^I, is composed of elements calculated as follows:

$$(3.8) \qquad \bar{\sigma}_{ij}^{I} = \frac{1}{N-1} \sum_{t=1}^{N} \left(\frac{y_{it} - \bar{y}_i}{\bar{y}_i} \right) \left(\frac{y_{jt} - \bar{y}_j}{\bar{y}_j} \right)$$

where $\bar{y}_{it}$ and $\bar{y}_{jt}$ denote observations for period t corresponding to industries i and j; and $\bar{y}_i$ and $\bar{y}_j$ denote the arithmetic means of the respective series.

When $i = j$, (3.8) reduces to the unbiased estimate of the relative variance of industry j;

$$(3.9) \qquad (\bar{\sigma}_j^{I})^2 = \frac{1}{N-1} \sum_{t}^{N} \left(\frac{y_{jt} - \bar{y}_j}{\bar{y}_j} \right)^2$$

The square root of this relative variance is the coefficient of variation for the respective industry, or

$$(3.10) \qquad \bar{\sigma}_j^{I} = \left[\frac{1}{N-1} \sum_{t}^{N} \left(\frac{y_{jt} - \bar{y}_j}{\bar{y}_j} \right)^2 \right]^{\frac{1}{2}}$$

This industry-specific measure of dispersion suffers from the same defect noted above for the same measure applied to individual regions: It is biased toward those industries that have experienced greater rates of growth. All covariances calculated on the basis of this measure are similarly biased. In order to eliminate this bias, here as before, regression techniques were used to estimate the quadratic trend for each industry. The residuals from that trend were then used directly for the calculation of a detrended relative covariance matrix, Σ^{II}, each element of which was computed as follows:[7]

$$(3.11) \qquad \bar{\sigma}_{ij}^{II} = \frac{1}{N-2} \sum_{t=1}^{N} \left(\frac{y_{it} - \hat{y}_{it}}{\bar{y}_i} \right) \left(\frac{y_{jt} - \hat{y}_{jt}}{\bar{y}_j} \right)$$

where $\hat{y}_{it}$ and $\hat{y}_{jt}$ denote the predicted level of employment in industry i for period t given by an equation identical to (3.3) (quadratic trend regression) but pertaining to industry i and j, respectively.

---

7. The calculation of the variance-covariance matrices directly from the residuals from the regression equation of each industry series is equivalent to calculating them from the actual adjusted time series.

Finally, a comparable matrix of detrended and deseasonalized relative covariances was calculated using the residuals for each of the industries from a quadratic trend plus a (120×11) dummy block for deseasonalizing, as in (3.5). Each element of this third matrix, Σ^{III}, was computed as follows:

$$(3.14) \qquad \bar{\sigma}^{III}_{ij} = \frac{1}{N-2} \sum_{t=1}^{N} \left(\frac{y_{itm} - \hat{y}_{iym}}{\bar{y}_i} \right) \left(\frac{y_{jtm} - \hat{y}_{jtm}}{\bar{y}_j} \right)$$

where y_{itm} and y_{jtm} denote the predicted level of employment in industries i and j for period t (season m) given by an equation identical to (3.6) but pertaining to industries i and j.

The resulting set of relative covariance matrices, with 13,924 elements in each (7,403 distinct elements) are too large to reproduce here. The indices of relative fluctuation calculated for each of the 118 industries from each of the covariance matrices are given in Appendix Table A.3.3. They consist of the coefficients of variation corresponding to the diagonal elements of each matrix, the relative variances. The mean national employment levels, $\bar{y}_i$ and $\bar{y}_j$ in equations (3.12) through (3.14), are listed in Appendix Table A.3.4.

Lovell [30] has noted that y^a_{it}, the adjusted value of the observation corresponding in this case to period t for industry i, may be obtained from detrended or deseasonalized residuals merely by adding to them the mean of the original series, $\bar{y}_i$. Thus:

$$(3.12) \qquad y^a_{it} = (y_{it} - \hat{y}_{it}) + \bar{y}_i.$$

The covariance pertaining to unadjusted data was, from (3.8),

$$(3.8) \qquad \bar{\sigma}^I_{ij} = \frac{1}{N-1} \sum_{t=1}^{N} \left(\frac{y_{it} - \bar{y}_i}{\bar{y}_i} \right) \left(\frac{y_{jt} - \bar{y}_j}{\bar{y}_j} \right).$$

For the adjusted data, this would be, from (3.12),

$$(3.13) \qquad \bar{\sigma}^I_{ij} = \frac{1}{N-2} \sum_{t=1}^{N} \left(\frac{y^a_{it} - \bar{y}_i}{\bar{y}_i} \right) \left(\frac{y^a_{jt} - \bar{y}_j}{\bar{y}_j} \right)$$

$$= \frac{1}{N-2} \sum_{t=1}^{N} \left[\frac{(y_{it} - \hat{y}_{it} + \bar{y}_i) - \bar{y}_i}{\bar{y}_i} \right] \left[\frac{(y_{jt} - \hat{y}_{jt} + \bar{y}_j) - \bar{y}_j}{\bar{y}_j} \right]$$

$$= \frac{1}{N-2} \sum_{t=1}^{N} \left(\frac{y_{it} - \hat{y}_{it}}{\bar{y}_i} \right) \left(\frac{y_{jt} - \hat{y}_{jt}}{\bar{y}_j} \right)$$

hence, equation (3.11).

These three covariance matrices provided the basis for estimating the theoretical variability of the industrial structures in each region on the assumption that the covariability of individual industries is identical across the nation.

Note that this is a far weaker assumption than that made by Borts [3] when he assumed implicitly that all industries were producing only final goods. The effect, comparability of industries across the nation, is the same. The covariability of two industries within a region, one may hypothesize, is largely a function of their production and consumption interdependence. To the extent that any pair of industries has greater production interdependence through common income elasticities of demand, their covariance will be higher than that of industries with less interdependence. Borts' analysis assumed away all production interdependence within regions; here we include it indirectly.

The portfolio variances calculated for each of the 52 cities on this basis are given in Table 3.5 in coefficient of variation form. Three measures are listed: the coefficient of variation calculated from unadjusted data,

$$(3.15) \qquad \bar{\sigma}_p^{I^k} = \left(\sum_{j=1}^{J} \sum_{i=1}^{J} x_i^k x_j^k \sigma_{ij}^I \right)^{\frac{1}{2}}$$

where x_i and x_j denote the percentages of total estimated 1963 manufacturing employment of region k found in industries i and j, respectively;

the coefficient of variation calculated from detrended data,

$$(3.16) \qquad \bar{\sigma}_p^{II^k} = \left(\sum_{j=1}^{J} \sum_{i=1}^{J} x_i^k x_j^k \sigma_{ij}^{II} \right)^{\frac{1}{2}}$$

and the comparable measure for detrended and deseasonalized data,

$$(3.17) \qquad \bar{\sigma}_p^{III^k} = \left(\sum_{i=1}^{J} \sum_{j=1}^{J} x_i^k x_j^k \sigma_{ij}^{III} \right)^{\frac{1}{2}}$$

It is to the testing and decomposition of these indices that the entire empirical exercise is directed.

Three alternative measures of industrial diversification were also calculated from this same data to correspond to prior measures discussed in Chapter 1. First, the "ogive" measure was calculated on the basis of the 118 modified 3-digit SIC grouping used for calculation of the portfolio variances. The following formula, taken from Bahl [2], was used:

66

TABLE 3.5

Theoretical Indices of Relative Instability:
Coefficients of Variation of Industrial Portfolio Variances
for Alternative Data Sets
(column ranks in parentheses)

Metropolitan Region	$\bar{\sigma}_c$ I (unadjusted)	$\bar{\sigma}_c$ II (detrended)	$\bar{\sigma}_c$ III (detrended and deseasonalized)
1 Albany	.05116 (39)	.01866 (44)	.01895 (31)
2 Albuquerque	.08264 (9)	.03862 (5)	.03818 (2)
3 Allentown et al.	.06521 (23)	.02059 (39)	.02048 (27)
4 Atlanta	.05794 (34)	.02059 (38)	.02033 (28)
5 Baltimore	.06029 (27)	.01824 (45)	.01816 (38)
6 Baton Rouge	.02652 (52)	.01354 (51)	.01053 (51)
7 Binghamton	.08816 (3)	.02628 (13)	.02530 (14)
8 Buffalo	.06835 (20)	.02281 (27)	.02339 (19)
9 Chattanooga	.05160 (38)	.02143 (35)	.02086 (26)
10 Chicago	.08075 (12)	.02206 (33)	.02215 (21)
11 Dallas	.06757 (21)	.01916 (41)	.01867 (34)
12 Denver	.04984 (42)	.01811 (47)	.01557 (46)
13 Detroit	.07816 (15)	.02799 (11)	.02659 (9)
14 Erie	.08193 (10)	.02893 (9)	.02894 (8)
15 Fort Wayne	.08721 (4)	.02868 (10)	.02910 (7)
16 Fresno	.07076 (18)	.05142 (2)	.01891 (32)
17 Gary et al.	.06018 (28)	.03833 (6)	.03811 (3)
18 Great Falls	.04552 (44)	.03283 (7)	.03314 (4)
19 Greensboro et al.	.04353 (48)	.01758 (49)	.01628 (44)
20 Indianapolis	.07947 (13)	.02521 (18)	.02547 (12)
21 Knoxville	.05453 (37)	.02270 (28)	.02099 (25)
22 Lancaster	.06398 (25)	.02299 (26)	.02249 (20)
23 Los Angeles et al.	.07918 (14)	.02216 (32)	.02158 (22)
24 Miami	.05882 (32)	.02388 (24)	.01651 (42)
25 Minneapolis et al.	.07071 (19)	.01811 (48)	.01804 (40)

(continued)

(Table 3. 5 continued)

Metropolitan Region	$\bar{\sigma}_c^{\text{I}}$ (unadjusted)	$\bar{\sigma}_c^{\text{II}}$ (detrended)	$\bar{\sigma}_c^{\text{III}}$ (detrended and deseasonalized)
26 New York	.05866 (33)	.01822 (46)	.01547 (48)
27 Omaha et al.	.04551 (45)	.02220 (31)	.01314 (49)
28 Philadelphia	.05914 (30)	.01869 (43)	.01828 (36)
29 Phoenix	.08464 (7)	.02496 (20)	.02513 (15)
30 Pittsburgh	.04978 (29)	.03249 (8)	.03292 (5)
31 Portland	.05058 (41)	.02228 (30)	.01808 (39)
32 Racine	.08483 (6)	.02480 (22)	.02545 (13)
33 Reading	.06469 (24)	.02526 (17)	.02550 (11)
34 Rochester	.08626 (5)	.02637 (12)	.02147 (23)
35 Salt Lake City	.06388 (26)	.02172 (34)	.02137 (24)
36 San Diego	.07103 (17)	.02610 (14)	.02610 (10)
37 San Francisco et al.	.05906 (31)	.02066 (37)	.01729 (41)
38 San Jose	.11003 (1)	.04923 (3)	.03254 (6)
39 Savannah	.05480 (36)	.02555 (15)	.01602 (45)
40 Seattle et al.	.05583 (35)	.02252 (29)	.01889 (33)
41 Sioux Falls	.03167 (51)	.01874 (42)	.01169 (50)
42 Spokane	.04677 (43)	.02505 (19)	.02476 (16)
43 Stockton	.07477 (16)	.05710 (1)	.01901 (30)
44 Syracuse	.08089 (11)	.02370 (25)	.02387 (18)
45 Tacoma	.04501 (46)	.02555 (16)	.01863 (35)
46 Tampa et al.	.05107 (40)	.02463 (23)	.01651 (43)
47 Topeka	.03179 (50)	.00883 (52)	.00622 (52)
48 Trenton	.06577 (22)	.01987 (40)	.01991 (29)
49 Tucson	.08312 (8)	.03895 (4)	.03821 (1)
50 Utica et al.	.08945 (2)	.02486 (21)	.02424 (17)
51 Wilkes-Barre et al.	.04445 (47)	.02093 (36)	.01825 (37)
52 Winston-Salem	.04252 (49)	.01730 (50)	.01550 (47)
Mean	.06385	.02514	.02179
Standard Deviation	.01726	.00892	.00677

Source: Calculated from author's regional industrial structure estimates and national interindustry variance covariance matrices.

$$(3.18) \qquad Q = \sum_{j=1}^{118} \left(\frac{(x_j - x_j^*)^2}{x_j^*} \right)$$

where x_j again denotes the proportion of total estimated manufacturing
employment in a region employed in industry j, and
x_j^* is the "ideal" weight implicit in the measure, here 1/118 or
.00849.
the alternative measure based on deviations from the national average used by Florence [13] and Borts [3] was calculated using the average
employment level in each of 118 industries in the 52 sample regions as
the "national" average with respect to which squared deviations were calculated. The set of "national" averages employed is given in Appendix
Table A. 3. 4. The calculations were based on the formula (also taken
from Bahl)

$$(3.19) \qquad N = \sum_{j=1}^{118} \left(\frac{(x_j - x_j^{**})2}{x_j^{**}} \right)$$

where $x_j^{**} = \frac{1}{52} \sum_{k=1}^{52} x_j^k$.

The percentage of manufacturing employment in durable goods was
calculated for purposes of comparison with the work of Siegel [53] and
Cutler and Hansz [10]. All three measures are given in Table 3. 6 for
each of the sample regions.
It would have been particularly interesting to be able to compare
the above measures with one additional measure, Ullman and Dacey's
"minimum requirements" measure, also discussed in Chapter 1. The
magnitude of the computational problem involved in deriving estimates
of this measure for the sector and regions considered here was, unfor-
tunately, too great for the time constraints of this study. It is hoped
that a future study will include this comparison. The "minimum requirements" method, though not without conceptual difficulty (as noted in
Chapter 1), remains the most sophisticated alternative to the portfolio
variance that has been offered to this date.

ANALYSIS OF ALTERNATIVE INDICES

It was suggested in Chapter 1 that an ideal index of diversification
will be independent of structural characteristics of a region other than
the specific set of industries, their respective magnitudes, and the

TABLE 3.6

Alternative Measures of Industrial Diversification
(column ranks in parentheses)

	Metropolitan Region	Ogive Measure	National Average Measure	Percent Durable Measure
1	Albany	4.04304 (35)	4.41188 (27)	.44713 (36)
2	Albuquerque	4.07031 (33)	5.40755 (18)	.68552 (10)
3	Allentown et al.	1.31123 (48)	2.23068 (40)	.43899 (38)
4	Atlanta	3.65172 (38)	2.25324 (38)	.43413 (39)
5	Baltimore	1.27964 (50)	6.61493 (12)	.53110 (29)
6	Baton Rouge	4.05835 (34)	12.51580 (2)	.16089 (51)
7	Binghamton	1.25163 (51)	2.10504 (42)	.61747 (22)
8	Buffalo	1.31040 (49)	1.67845 (44)	.64828 (19)
9	Chattanooga	9.74353 (4)	5.15666 (21)	.45620 (35)
10	Chicago	2.25408 (44)	1.49748 (48)	.64837 (18)
11	Dallas	1.51776 (46)	3.30187 (34)	.53534 (28)
12	Denver	7.26162 (14)	1.51098 (47)	.44544 (37)
13	Detroit	3.72744 (37)	3.92184 (30)	.78685 (3)
14	Erie	7.52772 (13)	4.85124 (22)	.75302 (4)
15	Fort Wayne	4.04057 (36)	1.25454 (50)	.83407 (1)
16	Fresno	1.38925 (47)	3.76847 (32)	.36627 (42)
17	Gary et al.	2.75211 (40)	5.57066 (17)	.68721 (9)
18	Great Falls	9.74320 (5)	10.30160 (4)	.56387 (26)
19	Greensboro et al.	9.89449 (3)	7.54454 (7)	.33181 (45)
20	Indianapolis	7.88194 (12)	5.96583 (15)	.64726 (20)
21	Knoxville	2.38169 (43)	5.17860 (20)	.38523 (41)
22	Lancaster	8.49870 (9)	6.29376 (14)	.59923 (24)
23	Los Angeles et al.	6.12934 (20)	1.59553 (45)	.66443 (15)
24	Miami	4.39237 (30)	1.30974 (49)	.43281 (40)
25	Minneapolis et al.	2.11953 (45)	2.14704 (41)	.57078 (25)

	Metropolitan Region	Ogive Measure	National Average Measure	Percent Durable Measure
26	New York	5.08151 (25)	3.18344 (35)	.35745 (44)
27	Omaha et al.	13.14698 (2)	4.20539 (28)	.32270 (46)
28	Philadelphia	6.57790 (18)	3.96937 (29)	.47835 (34)
29	Phoenix	1.07777 (52)	4.72657 (25)	.70686 (7)
30	Pittsburgh	5.18822 (24)	1.95239 (43)	.80259 (2)
31	Portland	3.20165 (39)	3.36037 (33)	.51967 (30)
32	Racine	5.21972 (23)	9.48785 (5)	.72478 (6)
33	Reading	6.63096 (15)	2.24313 (39)	.50422 (32)
34	Rochester	4.77744 (27)	6.47101 (13)	.61333 (23)
35	Salt Lake City	6.13833 (19)	3.13262 (36)	.64986 (17)
36	San Diego	7.98961 (11)	5.23008 (19)	.69301 (8)
37	San Francisco et al.	2.41062 (42)	2.41822 (37)	.50974 (31)
38	San Jose	4.46467 (29)	6.97366 (10)	.68032 (11)
39	Savannah	14.18257 (1)	3.18830 (1)	.24986 (48)
40	Seattle et al.	9.61155 (6)	1.02637 (52)	.67362 (13)
41	Sioux Falls	5.28939 (22)	7.48024 (8)	.20128 (50)
42	Spokane	6.61082 (16)	6.64145 (11)	.67724 (12)
43	Stockton	8.08215 (10)	1.54701 (46)	.35875 (43)
44	Syracuse	4.27420 (32)	4.80278 (23)	.66160 (16)
45	Tacoma	8.99154 (8)	5.74399 (16)	.55814 (27)
46	Tampa et al.	2.42386 (41)	6.98429 (9)	.48001 (33)
47	Topeka	4.90620 (26)	3.88062 (31)	.10963 (52)
48	Trenton	6.59883 (17)	4.75650 (24)	.61979 (21)
49	Tucson	9.26147 (7)	7.67592 (6)	.66945 (14)
50	Utica et al.	5.59000 (21)	4.58280 (26)	.74383 (5)
51	Wilkes-Barre et al.	4.58406 (28)	1.14308 (51)	.23721 (49)
52	Winston-Salem	4.33664 (31)	11.38762 (3)	.30096 (47)

	Mean	5.36308	4.74198	.53415
	Standard Deviation	3.07071	2.93477	.17481

Source: Calculated from author's metropolitan employment structure estimates.

appropriate "differences" among them. If it were not independent of other structural characteristics, its usefulness for analyzing the inter-relationship of industrial structure and other characteristics of regions in determining relative instability would be greatly diminished. Most importantly, nonindependence would not permit precise determination of the relative significance of the industrial structure variable. In Table 3.7 we present some empirical evidence of the properties of six alternative indices with respect to major structural characteristics of the sample regions.

A number of inferences may be drawn from the table. First, it may be seen that the theoretical bias of $\bar{\sigma}_p^I$ (square-root of the relative portfolio variance calculated from unadjusted data) is substantiated by the significant correlation coefficient of .2793 with growth rates.[8] The correlation between all the remaining measures and respective growth rates, except the national average measure, is insignificant. For the national average measure, an inverse relationship of low signi-ficance is indicated, suggesting that the greater the growth rate the lower the value of that measure (the greater the indicated diversification).

With respect to the relationship between the various indices and two measures of regional size–population and manufacturing employment–all three portfolio measures show little relationship to size. (Note that this does not mean that there is no relationship between relative fluc-tuations and size; that remains to be analyzed through the empirical indices of instability.) Of the six relevant coefficients, only one is of even low significance. The ogive measure also appears independent of city size, but the national average measure is significantly related to both measures. This bias toward larger cities was postulated for both ogive and national average measures in Chapter 1 but appears here only in the case of the latter. In this latter case it may be inferred that the national average measure will indicate greater diversification merely on account of the larger size of a city.

The total number of industries in each region (those with employ-ment greater than zero) is another structural characteristic of some interest to understanding the various indices. As we noted in Chapter

---

8. Thanks to the convenience of SPSS [39], levels of significance for one-tailed tests are reproduced for each correlation coefficient in Table 3.7 and subsequent tables of correlation coefficients. We believe that this practice, when and where possible, is substantially more informative than merely noting which coefficients are and which may not be significantly different from zero at one or more arbitrarily chosen levels of significance. For the sake of rhetorical clarity and readability, however, we shall refer to any coefficient that is significant at .01 or less as "highly significant," to any significant at .011 to .05 as simply "significant," to any significant at .051 to .10 as "of low significance," and to any others as "insignificant."

TABLE 3.7

Empirical Properties of Alternative
Measures of Diversification
(Pearson correlation coefficients
with levels of significance in parentheses)[*]

	Growth Rate	Population	Manufacturing Employment	Total Number of Industries
$\bar{\sigma}$ I p	.2793 (.023)	.0901 (.263)	.1210 (.197)	.1001 (.236)
$\bar{\sigma}$ II p	.1557 (.136)	-.1901 (.089)	-.1780 (.104)	-.1771 (.104)
$\bar{\sigma}$ III p	-.0040 (.489)	-.1221 (.195)	-.0900 (.263)	-.0600 (.337)
Ogive	-.1489 (.147)	-.1467 (.150)	-.1502 (.144)	-.3407 (.007)
National Average	-.1953 (.083)	-.3045 (.015)	-.2944 (.018)	-.6240 (.001)
Percent Durable	.0771 (.294)	.0741 (.301)	.0884 (.267)	.3384 (.008)

*Calculated using the Statistical Package for the Social Sciences developed by Nie, Bent, and Hull [39]. Levels of significance listed as (.001) should be read as "less than or equal to (.001)."

1, diversification of portfolios composed of equally weighted independent industries was closely associated with simply increasing the total number of industries in the portfolio. Two of the alternative measures were also shown to depend heavily upon the classification scheme for industries and to weight alternative industries as equally different and independent. It can be seen here that these two, ogive and national average, are highly significantly correlated with the number of industries in each region. This empirical relationship tends to substantiate the strength of this characteristic of each: that they tend to weight industries by presence or absence according to predetermined classifications, giving inordinate weight to zero industries (those not present).

The highly significant and direct relationship between percentage durable and total number of industries suggests that the larger the number of industries, the larger the proportion in durable goods, and consequently the less diversified the respective economy is supposed to be.

Given these biases in the respective indices, it is nonetheless important to test their respective explanatory power in terms of observed instability in the sample set of regions. Table 3.8 lists the correlation coefficients between the three empirical measures of relative instability and the six measures of diversification. It is immediately apparent that the three portfolio variance measures are substantially more closely correlated with observed instability than any of the alternatives for any of the data sets. This relationship is reinforced by Table 3.9, which presents the summary statistics from two-variable regression equations for the same set of variables.

The implications of Table 3.8 are repeated in Table 3.9. Although T and F tests for all three of the portfolio variance equations demonstrate significant or highly significant relationships, in only three of the remaining nine equations are the T-statistics of even low significance and in only four of the nine are the F-statistics of even low significance. The empirical index based on unadjusted data is persistently the most difficult to explain for all but the last measure. (Note that the negative adjusted coefficients of determination actually correspond to very small positive unadjusted coefficients that were forced negative by adjustment for degrees of freedom.)

The adjusted coefficients of determination for these simple regression equations may be interpreted as unbiased estimates of the proportion of total variation in the dependent variable (here the index of observed instability), which is attributable to a linear relationship with the independent variable (here the various measures of diversification of industrial structure). For the main series, therefore, relative diversification as measured by the corresponding portfolio variance "explains, " in this sense, 42.2 percent of the variation in observed relative instability. For the unadjusted data series, the spurious variation introduced by the biases toward growth inherent in both measures has reduced this explanatory power significantly. For the deseasonalized data series, the reduction in explanatory power to 23.5 percent may be attributable either to spurious variation in the indices created by adjustment for degrees of freedom where no seasonality was present or, more plausibly, to regional variations in seasonality such that the theoretical measure of instability based on a single variance-covariance matrix underestimated seasonality in some cases and overestimated it in others. Furthermore, as will be noted in the section on potential sources of error, there are numerous possible sources of spurious variation in both independent and dependent variables that would tend to explain why the "unexplained residual" is not smaller.

TABLE 3.8

The Relationship between Instability
and Alternative Indices of Diversification
(Pearson correlation coefficients with
levels of significance in parentheses)

	Z_c^{I}	Z_c^{II}	Z_c^{III}
$\bar{\sigma}_p^{I}$	2644 (.030)	- - - -	- - - -
$\bar{\sigma}_p^{II}$	- - - -	.6580 (.001)	- - - -
$\bar{\sigma}_p^{III}$	- - - -	- - - -	.5000 (.001)
Ogive	-.0207 (.443)	.2617 (.031)	.3201 (.011)
National Average	-.0039 (.490)	.1631 (.125)	.2840 (.021)
Percent Durable	.1727 (.111)	.0833 (.279)	.2319 (.050)

Of the alternative measures of diversification, none was capable
of accounting for as much as 8.5 percent of the observed variation.
Although the ogive measure bore a relationship that was significant
and highly significant with respect to the main series and the deseasonalized series, respectively, the proportion of variation explained
was less than a third of that of the portfolio variance measures in the
best of the cases for the former. The insignificance of the relationship
developed here between percentage durable and observed instability
is particularly striking in view of the relationship claimed by Siegel
[53]. He reported that a comparable measure of explained variation,
the squared Spearman rank-correlation coefficient, suggested that
percentage durable accounted for 49 percent of the observed variation
in an index very similar to that used here.

TABLE 3.9

Summary Regression Results for Indices of Instability
and Alternative Measures of Diversification

	Dependent Variable	Independent Variable	Adjusted R = Squared	I Statistic	F Statistic
1	Z_c^I	$\bar{\sigma}_p^I$	.0513	1.938^b	3.7568^b
2	Z_c^{II}	$\bar{\sigma}_p^{II}$	.4216	6.179^c	38.1793^c
3	Z_c^{III}	$\bar{\sigma}_p^{III}$	.2350	4.083^c	16.6675^c
4	Z_c^I	Ogive	-.0196	-.150	.0200
5	Z_c^{II}	Ogive	.0499	1.920^a	3.6800^b
6	Z_c^{III}	Ogive	.845	2.390^b	5.7100^c
7	Z_c^I	National Average	-.0200	0.030	.0008
8	Z_c^{II}	National Average	.0071	1.170	1.3700
9	Z_c^{III}	National Average	.0807	2.100^a	4.3800^b
10	Z_c^I	Percent Durable	.0104	1.240	1.5400
11	Z_c^{II}	Percent Durable	-.0129	.590	.3500
12	Z_c	Percent Durable	.0349	1.690^a	2.8400

[a]"Of low significance," significant at .10 but not at .05.
[b]"Significant," significant at .05 but not at .01.
[c]"Highly significant," significant at .01.

Whether the explanatory power of industrial diversification as measured by the portfolio variance here is sufficient to justify (or reestablish the validity of) using industrial structure as a diversification instrument for stabilization policy will depend upon the preferences and alternative of the policy maker. It would appear doubtful that any other single factor can be expected to account for as much as 42 percent of the variation in a cross-section as amall as 52 cities. In the opinion of the author, such significance for the data series that were previously established as a priori the most important lends more-than-adequate credibility to a policy of careful diversification in order to stabilize regional economies.

The relationship of instability to structural characteristics, other than the industrial structure as explicit in the portfolio variance, may be analyzed by extended multivariate analysis. In Table 3.10 we present the summary statistics of regressions that added both growth rates and indices of size to the equations above to test whether they made significant additional contributions.

Observing the T-statistics to note whether the coefficients of the new terms are significantly different from zero, we find that by that criterion neither size nor rate of growth are significantly related to observed instability in the sense of improving significantly upon or altering the explanatory power of the portfolio variance. The only exception to this, in both cases, is found for the unadjusted data set. There, the bias toward growth inherent in both the empirical measure of instability and the portfolio measure of the same form swamps the latter into insignificance and swells the coefficient of determination spuriously. The origin of significant relationships for measures of absolute size with respect to this data set is unclear. It is clear, however, that the relationship does not hold for either of the a priori preferable data sets.

The conclusion that there appears to be a lack of significant relationship between size and instability must be qualified in at least one way. It may well be that the cities included in the sample here are, in general, too large for the effects postulated by Thompson [57] to be evident. It may well be that the diversification that he suggests will accompany growth occurs for growth only among much smaller cities than those included here.

Regional variations in the level of observed instability may be analyzed using dummy variables for various regional breakdowns. Regional differences in instability might be considered proxies for many areally specific characteristics not otherwise specified here, such as differing institutional characteristics (heavily unionized areas possibly tending to be more stable than nonunion areas because of greater difficulties or costliness of laying-off workers). It is the weakness of dummy variables that they pick up forms of variation without specifying their precise nature; it is their strength that they do not require precise quantification.

TABLE 3.10

Summary Regression Results for Indices of Instability,
Portfolio Variances, and Additional Structural Characteristics

	Dependent Variable	Independent Variables (T-statistics in parentheses)		Adjusted R-Squared	F Statistic
1	Z_c^I	$\bar\sigma p_{(2.21)}^b$ I	Population $(-2.05)^b$	.1085	4.10^b
2	Z_c^{II}	$\bar\sigma p_{(5.93)}^c$ II	Population $(-.86)$	.4185	19.36^c
3	Z_c^{III}	$\bar\sigma p_{(3.97)}^c$ III	Population (-1.20)	.2416	9.13^c
4	Z_c^I	$\bar\sigma p_{(2.33)}^b$ I	Mfg. Employment $(-2.38)^b$	.1325	4.89^c
5	Z_c^{II}	$\bar\sigma p_{(5.92)}^c$ II	Mfg. Employment (-1.06)	.4231	19.70^c
6	Z_c^{III}	$\bar\sigma p_{(4.01)}^c$ III	Mfg. Employment (-1.42)	.2503	9.51^c
7	Z_c^I	$\bar\sigma p_{(.590)}$ I	Growth Rate $(7.08)^c$	.5215	28.78^c
8	Z_c^{II}	$\bar\sigma p_{(6.38)}^c$ II	Growth Rate (-1.37)	.4316	20.36^c
9	Z_c^{III}	$\bar\sigma p_{(4.05)}^c$ III	Growth Rate $(-.80)$	.2295	8.59^c

[a] "Of low significance," significant at .10 but not at .05.
[b] "Significant," significant at .05 but not at .01.
[c] "Significant at .01.

78

TABLE 3.11

Regional Subdivision of the United States

Label	Regional Economics Division Equivalents[a]	Component States
1. North	New England	Connecticut, Maine, Massachusetts, New Hampshire, and Vermont
	Mideast	Delaware, Maryland, New Jersey, New York, and Pennsylvania
	Great Lakes	Illinois, Indiana, Michigan, Ohio, and Wisconsin
2. Southeast	Southeast	Alabama, Arkansas, Florida, Georgia, Kentucky, Louisiana, Mississippi, North Carolina, South Carolina, Tennessee, Virginia, and West Virginia
3. South	Southeast	(as above)
	Southwest	Arizona, New Mexico, Oklahoma, and Texas
4. West	Southwest	(as above)
	Far West	Alaska, California, Hawaii, Nevada, Oregon, and Washington
	Rocky Mountain	Colorado, Idaho, Montana, Utah, and Wyoming

[a]Adapted from "Regions of the United States Used by Regional Economics Division, U.S. Department of Commerce," [40, p. 134].

TABLE 3.12

Summary Regression Results for Indices of Instability,
Portfolio Variances, and Regional Dummy Variables

	Dependent Variable	Independent Variables (T-statistics in parentheses)		Adjusted R-Squared	F Statistics
1	Z_c^{I}	$\bar{\sigma}_p$(3.92)^c	Northeast (-4.93)^c	.3529	14.91^c
2	Z_c^{II}	$\bar{\sigma}_p$(6.26)^c	Northeast (-2.39)^b	.4715	23.75^c
3	Z_c^{III}	$\bar{\sigma}_p$(5.06)^c	Northeast (-3.07)^c	.3454	14.45^c
4	Z_c^{I}	$\bar{\sigma}_p$(1.96)^a	West (2.76)^c	.1620	5.93^c
5	Z_c^{II}	$\bar{\sigma}_p$(5.20)^c	West (2.03)^b	.4559	22.36^c
6	Z_c^{III}	$\bar{\sigma}_p$(3.97)^c	West (2.78)^c	.2667	10.27^c

[a] "Of low significance," significant at .10 but not at .05.
[b] "Significant," significant at .05 but not at .01.
[c] "Highly significant," significant at .01.

A set of zero-one dummies was prepared for four major regions according to the Department of Commerce's Regional Economics Office regionalization of the United States. The four regions, dubbed Northeast, Southeast, South, and West, are identified in Table 3.11. The results of some of the regressions that added these dummies to the diversification indices are displayed in Table 3.12. It may be inferred from the statistics that, ceteris paribus, observed instability was significantly greater in the West than in the rest of the country as a whole and significantly less in the Northeast than in the rest of the country as a whole. That is, over and above the variation in instability accounted for by relative diversification, significant and remarkably different patterns of instability characterize the Northeast and the West. No comparable significant relationships were found for either the Southeast or the South, and the regression results are not presented.

Analysis of the specific sources of this differing regional instability is beyond the scope of this study. It is interesting merely to note that it does exist and does provide specific direction for extensions of the present study.

POTENTIAL SOURCES OF ERROR

The analysis undertaken here may be viewed in part as the testing of a definition. That is, if all data were perfectly accurate, all indices perfectly representative, and all calculations perfectly done, then the hypothesis in question reduces to the question, "To what extent is the actual instability of a region predicted by the weighted individual instability of—and the interdependence among—the set of industries present in that region?" If it is explained fully, that is, if no other factors determine relative instability, then the observed instability would be equal to the structurally predicted instability by definition. If the question is asked, as we have asked here, "To what extent does that structure account for the instability observed?", errors in measurement of any of the variables will tend to misrepresent the true explanatory power of the industrial structure.

There would appear to be greater likelihood that such errors of specification and measurement will tend to understate the explanatory power of the industrial structure rather than to overstate it. For the likelihood of random errors producing variations in the data of such a nature that it enhances the explanatory power of a variable as complex and as narrowly defined as the industrial structure as here interpreted seems very small by comparison with the probability of variations of any sort other than that. Every effort has been made, furthermore, to eliminate systematic bias toward the principal hypothesis. Several specific sources of potential spurious variation should be noted in evaluating the evidence presented here.

The basic regional employment data series, as noted above, were imprecise in several ways noted above and were not fully comparable to the national data series from which industry variances and covariances were calculated. For those regions in which definitional changes in geographic boundaries had been made, the estimation techniques for revising statistics to cover newly added counties have not been standardized by the Bureau of Labor Statistics and are a function of the sometimes sparse previously gathered data and the ingenuity of the statisticians in the cooperating state agencies.

The industrial structure estimates based on plant location data are likely to be the greatest single source of error. Although, as we noted, tests of the estimates that were possible indicate a generally good quality of the aggregate estimates, small variations in the estimated relative size of individual industries may make large contributions to error in statistics such as the portfolio variances where those errors in weights have been repeatedly multiplied through the variance-covariance matrices. One very specific form of error was unavoidably introduced in moving from the 144 3-digit industry groups for which employment was estimated from plant location data to the 118 industry groups for which time series were available. One category among the 144 consists of "Administrative and auxiliary" plants, establishments that do not actually produce manufactured goods at the specific site in question but rather provide administrative services to more than one manufacturing industry. Though such plants are frequently not assigned to specific industries at the local level, they are incorporated into one or another producing industry at the national level. The magnitude of this "industry" varied in the sample regions from zero to 36 percent of total estimated employment. The precise respective figures are given in Appendix Table A. 3. 5. Since no time series data are available for identifying the relative instability of this industry, some provision for this discrepancy had to be made. The solution chosen was to use the estimates for all industries based on percentage of total employment including Administrative and auxiliary. For cities with employment in this "industry," therefore, the vector of relative industrial weights does not sum to one. The effect is that of assuming that this industry varies with the average of all the rest, implicitly distributing employment over all other local industries in proportion to their relative magnitude. The alternative approach, recalculating all industry weights on the basis of total employment net of Administrative and auxiliary is conceptually equivalent to assuming that employment in that sector is invariant. This alternative approach was implemented through the stage of calculating Pearson correlation matrices such as those of Tables 3. 7 and 3. 8. The results consisted of almost uniformly lower correlation coefficients without altering the conclusions reached here on the basis of those tables.

The estimation of detrended or detrended and deseasonalized indices of instability for both regions and industries introduces error in that the regression equations provided, in most cases, good but not

82

perfect fit. To the extent, for example, that the true trend in any of such series was exponential or n^{th} order polynomial (and $n > 2$), the use of quadratic trends introduces error in the measurement of the instability of even the specific form defined. Presumably the estimation techniques chosen will minimize that error, but any error that remains will move us further from the definitional equality that might prevail in its absence.

Finally, the assumption that the variance-covariance matrix of employment in alternative industries was identical for all regions, although a necessary assumption given data limitations, is likely to have introduced further spurious variation.

It is not unreasonable to expect that detailed analysis at the level of individual regions utilizing unpublished local industrial time series would be likely to reduce the magnitude of all four types of measurement and specification error. Reduction of that error at the local level offers the best prospect for increasing the explantory significance of the portfolio variance and for testing more definitively the significance of the industrial structure variable in general.

4

SPATIAL EQUILIBRIUM, REGIONAL INDUSTRIAL DIVERSIFICATION, AND RATIONAL LOCATION SUBSIDIES

The first three chapters of this study have been oriented to problems of concept and measurement in the analysis of regional industrial diversification. In this chapter we explore, very briefly and somewhat superficially, the relationship between market location processes and industrial diversification as seen from the industrial portfolio point of view.

It is suggested here that differences in regional stability are likely to be associated with differences in the nominal wages paid among regions in spatial equilibrium. Those differences in wages are shown to be a function of relative regional industrial diversification. The possibility that the expansion or acquisition of a diversifying industry will lead to a reduction in equilibrium nominal wages for all employers in a region is presented as evidence of the existence of a new class of pecuniary regional externalities that provide a rational basis for regional subsidy to expansion or new location of the diversifying industry. A quasi-market procedure for the allocation of such subsidies is also suggested.

SPATIAL EQUILIBRIUM IN THE LABOR MARKET UNDER UNCERTAINTY

Within a determinate competitive framework the location decision of the economically rational individual laborer, at the level of choice among alternative regions, consists of choosing that region within which the stream of income will be greatest. [1]

---

1. It is clear that such a stream will be discounted to the time of decision, but in that which follows discounting will be ignored. Introduction of discounting creates algebraic complexity without altering the conclusions.

Let us assume that the cost of living is identical in all of a given set of regions among which an individual is making a location decision. Assume also that the individual is indifferent to nonpecuniary benefits of alternative regions and that initial moving costs are zero or otherwise negligible. Assume further that nonwage income for that individual is either zero or invariant with the location of his residence (dividends and rents not requiring his presence). Choice among regions is then a simple function of wage income. The individual will locate in that region which provides the greatest wage income and will relocate whenever greater wage income becomes available elsewhere. Spatial equilibrium of the labor force will occur when the labor force is distributed among regions in such a way that nominal income is identical in all.

Let us now alter the conditions of the analysis by introducing uncertainty in the labor market. Assume that final demand for the products of the various regions fluctuates over time in patterns that have different amplitude, and that are known only stochastically, in different regions. The derived demand for labor will also fluctuate. Even though nominal wages are known and identical in all regions, the stream of income to the individual laborer in each region will be known only as a probability distribution. To the extent that an individual is risk-averse, in the sense formalized by Arrow [1], the location choice among regions will be a function of not only the expected value of the income stream but also of the second and higher moments of the respective probability distributions on income.

Labor income under uncertainty can be divided into two components: a certainty-equivalent income and a risk-premium income. The certainty-equivalent income for a particular region and occupation is that income necessary to induce the supply of a given quantity of labor of a specific form when paid with probability 1.0. A contracted salary is a certainty-equivalent income. Most wage incomes are paid with certainty for those days or hours on which work is demanded, but the total wage-hours per unit of time, say a year, is not certain. To the extent that this labor demand is more variable over time, a higher risk premium must be added to the certainty-equivalent income in order to bring forth the labor needed when and where needed.

There are numerous examples available of relatively high and relatively low risk premiums. Civil service personnel in the United States have perennially taken relatively low hourly wages in return for considerable security, that is, freedom from variation in the annual incomes such wages generate. Skilled craftsmen must be paid more to work in the highly risky construction industry (even those such as trim carpenters who suffer none of the physical risks) rather than work in mass-production factory conditions with much less volatile demand.

The magnitude of the risk premium is a function of the magnitude of the risk aversion of the individual, the form in which that risk aversion enters his utility function, and the relative magnitude of the variability of income for the specific occupation and region. Whatever the form of the utility function, the relevant consideration for the risk-averse individual is the risk-compensated expected income, the sum of certainty-equivalent and risk-premium incomes.

For an individual with occupation i, expected income in region k may be expressed as:

$$(4.1) \qquad E(y_k^i) = \sum_t p_k^{ti} \, \bar{y}_k^{ti}$$

where: $\bar{y}_k^{ti}$ denotes the mean income per day or week of persons in k with occupation i and employed in industry t, and

p_k^{ti} denotes the probability of that individual being employed in industry t in region k. (It is a function of the relative size of t, the occupational requirements of t, and relative demand conditions in t.)

Let us assume that once a person has been "employed" in an industry, the principal source of variation in y_k^i is attributable to the daily or weekly duration of that employment, with the possibility of either exceeding or falling short of a standard work day or week.

If unemployment compensation is available, then expected income becomes:

$$(4.2) \qquad E(y_k^i) = Y_t^i = \sum_t p_k^{ti} \, \bar{y}^{ti} + (1 - \sum_t p_k^{ti}) \, c_k$$

where c_k denotes the region-specific unemployment compensation rate per day or week.

So long as the individual is risk averse, however, that expected income must be adjusted by the relative level of risk associated with it. Let us assume that the variance of the probability distribution on income offers an acceptable index of that risk. The variance of the distribution on income for the specific individual, assuming unemployment compensation invariant, may be written:

$$(4.3) \qquad \text{Variance } (y_k^i) = \sum_t p_k^{ti} \, \xi_k^{ti} + \sum_t \sum_s p_k^{ti} \, p_k^{si} \, \xi_k^{tsi}$$

where u_k^{ti} is the intertemporal variance on income for those of occupation i employed in industry t in region k, and

u_k^{tsi} denotes the covariance over time in region k between incomes of those in occupation i in industry t and comparable workers in industry s.

If we assume fixed coefficients of production, then fluctuations in final demand will lead to identical variance across occupations within an industry, hence the variance on income may be written:

$$(4.4) \qquad \text{Variance } (y_k^i) = \hat{\xi}_k^i = \sum_t \xi_k^t p_k^{ti} + \sum_t \sum_s p_k^{ti} p_k^{si} \xi_k^{ts}$$

where ξ_k^t denotes the variance on income for all occupations in industry t of region k, and

ξ_k^{ts} denotes the comparable covariance.

Note that from either (4.3) or (4.4) we may infer that the variability of wage income in any region for persons in any occupation is a function of not only the variability of a single industry, but also of any industry for which there is nonzero probability of employment—that is, a large subset of or possibly the entire set of principal industries in a region.

The risk-compensated real income of such an individual may be expressed as a function of the mean value of income and the variance of that income. Risk may enter the utility function in many ways. For the sake of simplicity, let us assume that expected returns and the variance determine risk-compensated income in the linearly risk-averse form suggested by Markowitz [32]. Then the expected value of the risk-compensated income for the individual with occupation i, ξ_k^i, will be

$$(4.5) \qquad \hat{\xi}_k^i = \xi_k^i + \lambda_k^i (\hat{\xi}_k^i - \bar{\xi}^i)$$

where λ_k^i denotes a risk-aversion parameter specific to region and occupation, and

$\bar{\xi}^i$ denotes the mean variance across regions for wage incomes of persons with occupation i.

The positive sign on the risk-aversion term reflects the fact that for spatial equilibrium in the labor market, y_k, the certainty-equivalent income may be the same in every region but $\hat{y}_k^i$ will be higher in those regions for which the variance of income is larger. To the extent that the variance of the expected stream of income can be reduced, the risk premium component of equilibrium wages will be reduced and the level of nominal wages may fall without any loss in welfare. To the extent that wage levels are a significant component of regional relative cost structures, reduction in the variability of income in a region will increase regional competitiveness.

The risk-premium income for an individual of occupation i in region k is, from equation (4.5):

$$(4.6) \qquad q_k^i = \lambda_k^i (\hat{\xi}_k^i - \bar{\xi}^i).$$

The total risk-premium income for region k is thus:

87

(4. 7) $$q_k = \sum_i \alpha_k^i \, q_k^i$$

where α_k^i denotes the proportion of total employed individuals in region k who are in occupation i.
That is, from (4. 6),

(4. 7') $$q_k = \sum_i \alpha_k^i \, \lambda_k^i \, (\hat{\xi}_k^i - \bar{\xi}^i).$$

The total risk-premium income is a function of the occupational distribution of the labor force, relative aversion to risk, and relative regional variability of wage incomes for each occupation that, as we have noted above, may be a function of the variability of all industries in a region and of their covariability. The most important consideration for that which follows is that, once again, the risk-premium income necessary to retain labor in spatial equilibrium under the uncertainty postulated is, for any occupation and hence for all individuals, a function of the fluctuations of most, if not all, industries in the region. Any reduction in the aggregate fluctuations will reduce the risk-premium wages necessary to retain the labor force.

REGIONAL INDUSTRIAL DIVERSIFICATION AND DIVERSIFICATION EXTERNALITIES

As developed in the preceding chapters, regional industrial diversification may be viewed as a process in which the aggregate variability of the "returns" that a region derives from its "portfolio" of economic activities among which regional productive resources are allocated. The portfolio approach to the analysis of regional industrial structure ("industrial" in the broad sense) serves to emphasize not only the stochastic nature of the returns to the region, but also the inherent interdependence among industries and their levels of activity attributable to interindustry production linkages and common patterns of demand for final products.

The approach also yields a formulation of the determinants of expected regional income and the variance of regional income that is convenient for purposes of considering relative fluctuation in wages. If we view the returns to be derived from an industrial portfolio as the total (or per capita) regional wage income to be derived from the set of industries producing in the region, then total risk-premium income for the region will be directly related to the portfolio variance of the set of industries in the area. That is, from equations (2. 45) and (4. 7'),

$$(4.8) \qquad q_k = \sum_i \alpha_k^i \lambda_k^i \left(\bar{\sigma}_p^K - \sum_k^K \sigma_p^k / k \right).$$

Diversification of any region k will lead, so long as it is greater than mean diversification nationwide, to a decrease in the risk-premium income required to obtain or retain the labor force in that area. From the point of view of producers in the region, diversification thus reduces the nominal wages they must pay. From the point of view of the labor force, there is no loss. For the reduction is solely related to the reduction in risk relative to other regions. There may be differential distribution of the effects of such a change if there were differences among members of the labor force in their aversion to risk. In that case, those members with the smallest aversion to risk would have been receiving greater certainty equivalent wages prior to diversification and might lose some of those after diversification and the consequent readjustment of wages. On average, however, the welfare gains and losses among laborers should net to zero.

The gains to all producers in the region are unambiguous. Lower nominal wages mean lower costs, assuming constant quality of labor, whatever the source of the reduction in wages. Whether market processes will lead toward the greatest possible reduction in risk premium wages, given regional variation in other costs of production and transport, will depend upon the availability of information on potential diversifying impact and upon the ability of firms to internalize their full effect upon regional wage levels.

It would appear unlikely that information on the diversifying impact of most location decisions is currently known and incorporated in those decisions. If the effects on the risk-premium wage were fully known prior to the location decision, will market location processes lead new or expanded plants to those regions where, ceteris paribus, their diversifying impacts will be the greatest? Assume that the owners of a firm are selecting the region within which to locate a new plant, that among a certain set of K contiguous candidate regions capital costs are identical and differences in total transportation costs are similarly negligible. The location decision for such a plant will depend upon the relative nominal wages. Assume further that the existing industrial structures among the K regions differ substantially, so the diversifying potential of the new plant varies across the regions. Let price levels, nonpecuniary benefits, and nonwage income be invariant across the K regions. Nominal wages, in spatial equilibrium, will then differ only by the risk-premium differences attributable to relative regional industrial portfolio variances. Now consider two cases.

Consider first the case in which the portfolio variances are coincidentally identical. Nominal wages will be equal across all regions. In this case the new plant will be located in that region within which its diversifying impact will be greatest, for in that region the derived reduction in risk-premium wage will provide the plant with its lowest risk-compensated nominal wage costs.

Consider the second case, however, in which portfolio variances are not coincidentally the same. In such a case the new plant would locate in that region in which the prior nominal wage, less the effect of its diversifying impact upon the risk-premium wage, is minimized. This decision is as likely to be destabilizing as it is to be diversifying or stabilizing. For if a region upon which the new location would have a destabilizing effect happened to have a prior nominal wage less than the other regions by more than the wage increase induced by destabilization, the plant would be located in that region despite the deleterious effects.

It is clearly possible that regions would choose to accept industries that increase instability if they simultaneously increase income levels by enough to offset the increased instability at the rate indicated by the risk aversion parameter. But there is no rationale for choosing or permitting the location of plants that increase the pure risk-premium wage without compensating benefits. Market location processes may lead to such a result.

This phenomenon is evidence of the existence of a class of external effects of the location of an industry within a region that has not heretofore been examined. An industry that will tend to diversify a region will be capable of internalizing only those benefits from the diversifications that accrue in terms of the reduced nominal wages that it will be required to pay. The reduction in nominal wages that all other employers in that region may pay and still retain their labor force will accrue as pecuniary external benefits. Conversely, the location of a destabilizing plant may be rational from the point of view of the individual plant, because it is required to internalize less than the total increase in nominal wages that its location decision implies for all producers in the region.

The creation of contingent claim markets is frequently offered as a method for internalizing the failure of other markets to cope adequately with the effects of uncertainty. In this case a nationally pooled (or otherwise supraregionally pooled) unemployment compensation program could serve this purpose if compensation were raised to levels that would be realistic substitutes for wage income. The current system of locally or regionally financed unemployment compensation programs fails to perform this function. Since unemployment insurance rates that must be paid by employers in most areas are tied to local or state unemployment experience, the acquisition of a destabilizing industry will raise full labor costs partly through increased risk-premium wage and partly through the increased insurance rates necessary to maintain the compensation programs actuarially sound. In the absence of appropriate pooling and given the practical and political objections to unemployment compensation levels that approach wage income levels, there is need for efficient intervention in market location processes.

A QUASI-MARKET ALLOCATION PLAN
FOR DIVERSIFICATION SUBSIDIES

The existence of diversification externalities implies that subsidies to the expansion of or the new location of diversifying industries may be rational from the point of view of all other producers in a region in order to reduce the risk-premium wage that each must pay. In the presence of perfect information, the calculation of the maximum rational subsidy and the minimum necessary subsidy would be straightforward and bargaining between representatives of the region and representatives of the plant would determine the actual magnitude of the subsidy.

In a real world context of far-less-perfect information, one in which firms are unlikely to know of their potential for stabilizing or destabilizing income in a region and in which regional representatives are unlikely to know of all firms that might locate plants within their region, a different approach will be required.

A procedure that required that industries "bid" on a finite quantity of diversification subsidies would force the revelation of the information necessary to choose those industries most likely to produce the desired effects. Let those industries that are interested in receiving location subsidies submit a "bid" consisting of a description of the size and occupational structure of the labor force to be employed, the levels of wages to be paid, and the nature of products to be produced. The bidding firm would also be required to submit a statement of the minimum subsidy (per year or per unit of output) necessary to induce it to locate in the given region.

Simulation of diversifying effects of the proposed plant upon the industrial portfolio variance for the region, using techniques such as those suggested in Chapter 5, would then permit estimation of the magnitude of the derived reduction in risk premium wage as returns from the subsidy. The maximum rational subsidy (per year or unit of output) could then be calculated. Alternative bidders could then be ranked on the basis of the ratio of returns to subsidy. Subsidies could be extended to those plants with the greatest returns to the subsidy until the declared total subsidy had been allocated, or until the returns to subsidy ratio reached 1.0. It is likely that actual payment of the subsidy should be linked to fulfillment of the employment or output levels promised in the bids. The possibility that some of the plants receiving subsidies might have located in the region without the subsidy simply means that industries that would have created external benefits through subsidy-free location are receiving some share of those benefits.

5

ALTERNATIVE STRATEGIES
FOR REGIONAL INDUSTRIAL
DIVERSIFICATION

The conversion of the theoretical approach to industrial diversification into a useful operational tool requires consideration of techniques for implementing the approach at the local level. In this chapter we consider the problem of choosing an optimally diversifying increment to regional industrial structures. Three alternative approaches or "strategies" for choosing such increments are explored, first theoretically and then in terms of their significance for three U.S. cities that have had histories of instability greater than average for comparable cities.

In the first section we consider the extension of the industrial portfolio approach to the specific problem of choosing increments to a given industrial structure. In the second section empirical analysis of the suggested optimally diversifying increments for the three cities affords an opportunity to compare and constrast the alternative strategies in terms of their policy implications for these and other cities.

ALTERNATIVE STRATEGIES FOR CHOOSING
DIVERSIFYING INCREMENTS

Seeking Nationally Stable Industries

Given an industrial structure that is considered by policy makers to possess excessive instability, and given an interest in seeking and encouraging the location of diversifying increments to that industrial structure, some procedure is required for identifying and evaluating alternative candidate diversifying industries. The simplest procedure (and that which is implicit in the pessimistic comments of Thompson and Richardson noted in Chapter 1) would consist of identifying those individual industries that have demonstrated the greatest stability (or the least variability) with respect to the returns criterion that one is using and of increasing as much as possible the relative magnitude of such industries in the given industrial structure. The conventional wisdom that one should seek nondurable-goods industries rather than durable-goods industries is consistent with this approach, for such advice is generally predicated on the assumption that durable-goods industries will be less stable and that such individual-industry considerations are those that are relevant.

In an industrial portfolio context, however, the only time when consideration of individual industry characteristics is appropriate occurs when interindustry interdependence is either nonexistent or so small as to be negligible. The standard theorems of portfolio diversification suggest, however, that even in this case optimal diversification consists not of unlimited increments of the most stable industry but rather of movement toward identical quantities of all industries [see 21, 22].

Given interdependence in either the production or the consumption of the products of potential diversifying industries and/or the existing industrial structure, a more reasonable assumption than its contrary, there remains the fundamentally empirical question of whether such interdependence is great enough to invalidate a procedure of simply increasing the relative magnitude of the least variable industries.

Systematic Simulation of Sets of Industry Increments

Let us assume, for the moment, that such interdependence proves empirically significant. How does one then choose optimally diversifying increments? Two procedures are possible. The first consists of simulating the addition of alternative industrial increments and then calculating their relative impacts upon the index of aggregate regional instability, the regional industrial portfolio variance. Such a simulation technique offers the advantage of incorporating directly the interdependence among existing industries, their relative existing magnitude, and any specific set of proposed industry increments. For an increment of Δ in industry k, say Δ_k, the simulation of its impact upon aggregate regional instability could consist of the following set of calculations.

$$(5.1) \qquad P_{\Delta_k} = \frac{\left(\sum_{i,j} \hat{w}_i \hat{w}_j \, \sigma_{ij} \right) - \left(\sum_{i,j} w_i w_j \, \sigma_{ij} \right)}{\left(\sum_{i,j} w_i w_j \, \sigma_{ij} \right)}$$

where P_{Δ_k} denotes the percentage change in aggregate regional instability attributable to an increase of magnitude Δ in industry k;

w_i and w_j denote the relative weight (or magnitude) of industry i and j;

$\hat{w}_i$ and $\hat{w}_j$ denote the adjusted relative weights of industries i

and j after industry k has been expanded absolutely by Δ_k; and σ_{ij} denotes the covariance of the returns criterion between industry i and industry j.

If the relationship between P_{Δ_k} and Δ_k were linear, the simulation approach would gain impressive power. For then it would be possible to estimate the diversifying impact of a small increment of each potential industry and to project alternative weighted combinations of industrial increments on that basis. The relationship however can be shown to be nonlinear; and the simulation approach is greatly weakened as a result.

To derive an explicit function for the relationship between P_{Δ_k} and Δ_k, let us incorporate Δ_k explicitly in equation (5.1). Let H be the total quantity of resources allocated to all industry in a given region at the time of choosing among potential diversifying increments. Let h_j be the quantity of resources allocated to industry j in that same base period, and let Δ_k represent the total planned increment in allocable resources, here assumed to be allocated to a single industry k. Then the following substitutions may be made in (5.1)

(5.2a) $\qquad w_i = \dfrac{h_i}{H}, \quad w_j = \dfrac{h_j}{H}, \quad$ for all i and j

(5.2b) $\qquad \hat{w}_i = \dfrac{h_i}{H + \Delta_k}, \quad \hat{w}_j = \dfrac{h_j}{H + \Delta_k}, \quad$ for all i and j $\neq$ k

(5.2c) $\qquad \hat{w}_k = \dfrac{h_k + \Delta_k}{H + \Delta_k}, \quad$ for any k.

Isolating the influence of industry k, we may rewrite (5.1) as:

(5.1') $\qquad P_{\Delta_k} = \dfrac{\left(\sum\limits_{i,\,j \neq k} \sigma_{ij} \hat{w}_i \hat{w}_j + 2 \sum\limits_{j \neq k} \sigma_{jk} \hat{w}_j \hat{w}_k + \sigma_k^2 w_k^2 \right) - \sum\limits_{i,j} \sigma_{ij} w_i w_j}{\sum\limits_{i,j} \sigma_{ij} w_i w_j}.$

Substituting (5.2a through c) into (5.1'), we obtain,

(5.1'') $\qquad P_{\Delta_k} = \dfrac{\sum\limits_{i,\,j \neq k} \sigma_{ij} \left[\dfrac{h_i}{(H+\Delta k)} \dfrac{h_j}{(H+\Delta k)} \right] + 2 \sum\limits_{j \neq k} \sigma_{jk} \left[\dfrac{h_j}{(H+\Delta k)} \dfrac{(h_k+\Delta k)}{(H+\Delta k)} \right]}{\sum\limits_{i,j} \sigma_{ij} \left(\dfrac{h_i}{H} \dfrac{h_j}{H} \right)}$

$\qquad\qquad + \dfrac{\sigma_k^2 \left(\dfrac{h_k+\Delta k}{H+\Delta k} \right)^2 - \sum\limits_{i,j} \sigma_{ij} \dfrac{h_i}{H} \dfrac{h_j}{H}}{\sum\limits_{i,j} \sigma_{ij} \left(\dfrac{h_i}{H} \dfrac{h_j}{H} \right)}$

94

Simplifying and resubstituting somewhat, this becomes

$$(5.1''')\qquad P_{\Delta_k} = \sum_{i,j \neq k} \sigma_{ij}\left[\frac{H^2}{(H+\Delta_k)^2}\right] + 2\sum_{j \neq k} \sigma_{kj}\left[\left(\frac{1}{w_k w_j}\right)\frac{h_k h_j + \Delta_k h_j}{(H+\Delta_k)^2}\right]$$

$$+ \sigma_k^2\left[\frac{(h_k+\Delta_k)^2}{(H+\Delta_k)^2}\right]$$

Thus the percentage change in aggregate regional instability is a complex nonlinear function not only of Δ_k, but also of the size of Δ_k relative to the total size of the regions's resources, of the previous relative weight of industry k, of the previous relative weight of all other preexisting industries, as well as of the covariances among industry k and all preexisting industries and the variance of k itself.

Such a result should not be surprising. For although a small increment of any industry may have some diversifying impact (unless that industry is already relatively large), continued increases in the relative magnitude of that industry move the industrial structure toward specialization in that industry and, consequently, toward ever-heavier weight attached to its variance and covariances. Unless the stability of that industry is unusually great or its covariances with preexisting industries large and negative, the industrial portfolio variance can be expected, ultimately, to rise with further additions of that industry.

Given that such nonlinearities exist, in order to select an optimal set of industrial increments one would need to run a very large number of simulations to take into consideration the varying impact of increases of each different size in each possible set of combinations of even a small number of alternative industries. The strength of the simulation approach appears, however, when one is faced, as is often the case in reality, with a very limited number of alternatives from among which to choose.

A Mathematical Programming Approach

If one wishes to derive a set of theoretically optimal diversifying increments to an existing regional structure, most of the difficulties encountered in the discussion of the simulation of alternative increments can be overcome by incorporating the full interrelationships into a nonlinear mathematical programming framework. This third strategy would be particularly appropriate under conditions where a regional planning authority was preparing to subsidize the location of new diversifying industry (or the expansion of existing industry) and was attempting to determine what industries to seek to attract (or to induce to expand).

If we continue to assume that the variance is an appropriate measure of the risk associated with an industry, the optimal trade-off between returns from industries and the risks of instability can be derived by quadratic programming with respect to the relative weights of all present and potential industries. As developed in Chapter 2, the maximization problem may be written as

$$(5.3) \qquad \underset{w}{\text{Max}} \ Z = \sum_j \hat{w}_j \mu_j - \lambda \sum_{i,j} \hat{w}_i \hat{w}_j \sigma_{ij}$$

subject to:

$$(5.3a) \qquad \hat{w}_j \geq b_j, \ \text{for all } j$$

$$(5.3b) \qquad \sum_j \hat{w}_j = \sum_j w_j + \Delta \ \text{and}$$

$$(5.3c) \qquad \hat{w}_j \geq 0, \ \text{for all } j$$

where $\hat{w}_j$ denotes the relative weight of industry j in the optimal port-folio of industries,

μ_j denotes the expected value of the returns criterion with respect to industry j;

λ denotes the negative weight associated with the instability or risk that is approximated by the second term. The greater the aversion of a region (through its policy makers) to instability in returns, the greater the value of λ and the heavier the rela-tive weight placed upon averting that instability.

The constraint set (5.3a) determines the treatment to be accorded to preexisting industries in the region. They may be structured as lower bounds, upper bounds, or strict equality requirements by varying the direction of the inequality and the relationship between b_j the constraint coefficient and w_j, the industry weight in the base period. For example, if b_j were set equal to $w_j = h_j/H$ in constraint set (5.3a), then the con-straint set would have the effect of retaining all preexisting industries (ignoring depreciation) at absolute levels of resource allocation at least comparable to current or base levels.

Constraint (5.3b) presents the total supply constraint with respect to allocable resources. The total increment in allocable resources, Δ, is shown to be equal to the sum of the individual industry increments in weight, that is

$$\sum_j (\hat{w}_j - w_j).$$

The programming formulation of the choice problem has several important disadvantages. First, it is necessary in this particular variant of it to assume that all industries are infinitely divisible into plants of varying sizes. A discrete programming formulation is also possible as noted in Chapter 2, but the specific information requirements become extremely cumbersome. An additional difficulty of the approach has to do with the feasibility from a location theory viewpoint of some increments in some industries. One cannot expect that any industry could be induced to locate in any region at levels of subsidy that are less than total benefits; and as further constraints on locational feasibility are added for each industry, the processing of the program becomes increasingly expensive. In the long run, as the number of alternative feasible industries, possible discrete scales, and other feasibility conditions reduce the feasibility set, the relative usefulness of the programming and the simulation strategies may be expected to converge.

AN APPLICATION OF THE ALTERNATIVE STRATEGIES
TO CONTEMPORARY DIVERSIFICATION PROBLEMS

The potential effectiveness of the alternative diversification strategies may be evaluated in part by a comparison of the results that they would produce when applied to the actual structures of current U. S. regions. Several fundamentally empirical questions may be asked in this context. Are the interindustry interdependencies of sufficient magnitude to invalidate or to weaken the applicability of the first strategy: expansion of the least variable industries? Is the absolute magnitude of the potential reduction in regional instability sufficient to warrant continued attention to regional industrial diversification efforts? Are the differences among the diversifying impacts of different industries of sufficient magnitude to warrant continued attention to an optimal set of increments rather than an arbitrary set? And are the differences among the policies dictated by the alternative strategies of sufficient magnitude to suggest one rather than another? The results of empirical analyses that are reported below suggest a strong but qualified "Yes" in response to each of these questions.

In order to seek answers to such questions it was possible to draw data from that derived for the analysis in Chapter 3. The matrix of detrended relative variances and covariances (Σ^{II}) provides, from its main diagonal, indices of individual industry national variability in employment in interindustrially comparable dimensions. The ten least-variable and the ten most-variable industries, according to this criterion, are listed in Table 5.1. The complete list is given in Appendix Table A. 3. 3, column 2.

In order to apply this industry data to diverse but comparable regions, three metropolitan regions were chosen, each reflecting a fundamentally different type of regional economy. All three are Standard Metropolitan Statistical Areas, and all three have experienced instability in their manufacturing employment, which was greater than average for comparable regions. Furthermore, each was found to have an industrial structure that could have been expected to have produced fluctuations greater than average.

TABLE 5.1

Comparative Industry Variability:
10 Least-Variable and 10 Most-Variable Industries
(based on coefficients of variation
of fluctuations around 120-month trend)

Rank	Combined Industry Group	Index
	Least-Variable Industries	
118 205	Bakery products	.01169
117 275	Commercial printing	.01178
116 274	Miscellaneous publishing	.01309
115 271	Newspapers	.01346
114 281	Industrial chemicals	.01444
113 264	Misc. converted paper products	.01623
112 265	Paperboard containers and boxes	.01652
111 291	Petroleum refining	.01685
110 384	Medical instruments and supplies	.01744
109 284	Soap, cleaners, and toilet goods	.01829
108 226	Textile finishing, except wool	.01845
	Most-Variable Industries	
1 204	Grain mill products	.23755
2 206	Sugar products	.20750
3 331	Blast furnace and basic steel products	.12085
4 394	Toys and sporting goods	.11187
5 241	Logging camps and contractors	.10606
6 374	Railroad equipment	.10535
7 19	Ordnance and accessories	.10417
8 287	Agricultural chemicals	.09632
9 321	Flat glass	.09468
10 365	Radio and TV receiving equipment	.08822

Source: Calculated by the author.

The first, Detroit, is representative of large, old, heavily industrial regions with considerable durable goods manufacturing. The second, Great Falls, Montana, is representative of a small region with relatively few industries and heavy reliance upon basic metals manufacture. More than 39 percent of its estimated 1963 manufacturing labor force was employed in nonferrous metals. The third region, Stockton, California, possesses an economy heavily specialized in highly seasonal food processing, especially fruit and vegetable packing. The complete distribution of 1963 manufacturing employment estimated for each of these three metropolitan regions across the same 118 3-digit combined industry groups as above is given in Appendix Table A. 5. 1.

As one can note from Tables 3. 2 and 3. 5, these three cities were characterized by relatively very high empirical and theoretical indices of instability in the context of the 52 SMSAs studied. The arithmetic mean for the 52 empirical indices was . 04705 (standard deviation, . 03444). Great Falls possessed the greatest empirical instability of the 52 with an index of . 19348; Stockton was second with . 17133; and Detroit was ninth (the highest of any large industrial city) with . 06063. In terms of the expected instability attributable to industrial structure, the mean of the 52 was . 02514 (standard deviation, . 00892). Stockton ranked first with . 05710, Great Falls was seventh with . 03283, and Detroit eleventh with . 02799.

Choice of Least-Variable Industries

The three alternative strategies for diversifying the given industrial structures were then applied to each of these three cities. First, single-industry increments of 5, 10, and 15 percent of the 1963 manufacturing labor force were simulated for each of the 118 industry groups. On the basis of the data generated in that way it is possible to reach preliminary conclusions about what increments in which industries will tend to produce the greatest reduction in the theoretical index of instability in each city and about the extent to which the greatest reductions are associated with the least variable industries as noted in Table 5.1.

The procedure consists of calculating $P_{\Delta k}$ from equation (5. 1) for the least-variable industries and for the most-variable industries over various values of Δ. The resulting figures for $P_{\Delta k}$ provide an indication of the extent to which aggregate instability in the industrial structure will be improved or worsened by the various Δ_k.

An understanding of their significance requires noting the specific significance of the portfolio variances with respect to which they are calculated. The index of instability calculated, for example, for Stockton (. 05710) may be related to the unemployment rate of the area. By selecting employment alone as the returns criterion with respect to which we analyze diversification, the theoretical index of instability is directly related to the extent to which actual employment has deviated (and, with a given industrial structure, can be expected to deviate) from its trend. Negative deviation from that trend will be tantamount to unemployment, positive deviation equivalent to undersupply of labor, so long as the labor force is assumed to grow along the long-run trend.

If positive and negative fluctuations are assumed to be normally distributed around that trend over time, then an index of . 05710 means, from the Z table, that there is approximately . 3174 probability that deviations will be greater than 5.71 percent of the mean. Given the symmetry of the normal distribution this may be interpreted to mean that there is .1587 probability of negative deviations (unemployment) being greater than 5.71 percent of the mean level in any month. Or, in more familiar terms, there is only .05 probability of unemployment exceeding 1.64 times the index of instability. For Stockton this would mean .05 probability of unemployment greater than 9.36 percent. A 10 percent reduction in the index of instability will thus mean a 16.4 percent reduction in the 5 percent probability unemployment rate, that is, in the case of Stockton a reduction from 9.36 to 7.83 percent.

The percentage changes in theoretical structural instability by various increments of the five least-variable and the five most-variable industries are presented in Table 5.2. It may be noted in that table that the least variable industries appear to reduce the index of instability by generally larger amounts than the most variable industries. At least two out of five of the most-variable industries worsen the index of instability in each city. More notable, however, are the inconsistencies that are apparent. For Detroit, increments in industry group 204, the most variable of all industries, would produce a greater reduction in aggregate instability than any of the five least-variable industries at all incremental sizes. For Great Falls, the same industry would reduce aggregate instability by roughly the same as the five least-variable industries. For both Stockton and Great Falls, industry group 206 would reduce instability at an incremental level of 5 percent but would increase instability by substantial amounts at 10 and 15 percent levels. This nonlinearity is further apparent in the case of Detroit. A 5 percent increase there in industry group 241 (one of the "most variable") will reduce aggregate instability by 4.6 percent, but a 10 or 15 percent increase would reduce instability by the increasing and then diminishing proportions of 5.5 percent and 3.7 percent respectively.

Systematic Simulation of Alternative Increments

The second strategy, suggested in part to internalize the relationships among industries and the preexistence of some industries, consisted of simulating systematically the impact of all potential alternative industries at various levels of increase. Rather than attempt to simulate all possible combinations of various increases in the 118 industry groups, the same three increases as above were simulated for all 118 industries in each. Percentage changes in the index of theoretical instability were calculated and ranked. The five "best" industries and the five "worst" industries according to this diversification criterion are listed in Table 5.3. The complete list of industry simulation results at all three levels of increase is given in Appendix Table A.5.2.

TABLE 5.2

Percentage Changes in Instability through Diversification According
to Strategy 1: Choose the Least-Variable and Avoid the Most-Variable Industries

Variability Rank	Industry Group	Percentage Change in Instability		
		$\Delta_k = 5\%$*	$\Delta_k = 10\%$*	$\Delta_k = 15\%$*
		Detroit		
118	205	-5.109	-9.716	-13.884
117	275	-4.309	-8.187	-11.693
116	274	-4.553	-8.643	-12.331
115	271	-4.184	-7.940	-11.323
114	281	-4.520	-8.579	-12.209
1	204	-5.832	-10.981	-15.532
2	206	+5.035	+18.794	+36.764
3	331	+4.947	+12.769	+20.548
4	394	-3.799	-3.769	-3.669
5	241	-4.575	-5.539	-3.669
		Great Falls		
118	205	-4.826	-9.186	-13.139
117	275	-4.877	-9.282	-13.277
116	274	-4.531	-8.615	-12.312
115	271	-4.362	-8.290	-11.845
114	281	-4.480	-7.152	-10.133

(continued)

101

TABLE 5.2 continued

Percentage Changes in Instability through Diversification According
to Strategy 1: Choose the Least-Variable and Avoid the Most-Variable Industries

Variability Rank	Industry Group	Percentage Change in Instability		
		$\Delta_k = 5\%$*	$\Delta_k = 10\%$*	$\Delta_k = 15\%$*
		[Great Falls]		
1	204	-4.492	-8.460	-11.976
2	206	-4.313	+0.321	+10.850
3	331	+1.076	+4.447	+9.337
4	394	-0.952	+0.454	+3.557
5	241	-2.184	-2.016	-0.075
		Stockton		
118	205	-4.201	-8.015	-11.491
117	275	-4.577	-8.724	-12.503
116	274	-4.231	-8.068	-11.563
115	271	-4.380	-8.351	-11.967
114	281	-4.380	-8.348	-11.960
1	204	-3.374	-6.422	-9.188
2	206	-0.122	+2.272	+6.408
3	331	-6.955	-12.269	-16.122
4	394	+3.070	+6.082	+9.000
5	241	+2.241	+4.533	+6.824

*Increments consist of 5, 10, and 15 percent of the 1963 total estimated manufacturing labor force. For Great Falls and Stockton these increments consist of 133, 266, 399, and 731, 1,462, and 2,193 employees in each case. For these regions growth of this magnitude is comparable to the new location of a medium to large new industrial plant. For Detroit the comparable employment increases are 22,580, 45,160, and 67,740 employees. Although it is clearly unrealistic to expect a single industry to grow by that magnitude in a short period of time, the same percentages were used for Detroit to preserve strict comparability.

Source: Calculated by the author.

TABLE 5.3

Percentage Changes in Instability through Diversification According to Strategy 2: Simulate and Rank Alternative Increments (ranked percentage changes in index of instability)

Rank	$\Delta_k = 5\%$ Industry Group	Percent Change	$\Delta_k = 10\%$ Industry Group	Percent Change	$\Delta_k = 15\%$ Industry Group	Percent Change
			Detroit			
1	203	-8.603	204	-10.981	204	-15.531
2	190	-7.116	190	-10.389	202	-14.281
3	204	-5.832	202	-10.139	205	-13.884
4	286	-5.481	205	-9.716	284	-13.685
5	202	-5.408	208	-9.664	208	-13.362
114	321	+4.285	321	+9.666	203	+18.071
115	331	+4.947	331	+12.138	331	+20.548
116	206	+5.035	374	+15.345	374	+23.620
117	374	+7.307	371	+17.125	371	+24.862
118	371	+8.837	206	+18.794	206	+36.764
			Great Falls			
1	190	-6.541	190	-10.186	272	-13.804
2	366	-5.396	272	-9.723	211	-13.469
3	301	-5.185	211	-9.499	275	-13.278
4	272	-5.146	366	-9.433	209	-13.180
5	211	-5.035	275	-9.282	205	-13.139

(continued)

(TABLE 5.3 continued)

Rank	$\Delta_k = 5\%$ Industry Group	$\Delta_k = 5\%$ Percent Change	$\Delta_k = 10\%$ Industry Group	$\Delta_k = 10\%$ Percent Change	$\Delta_k = 15\%$ Industry Group	$\Delta_k = 15\%$ Percent Change
			Great Falls			
114	344	-0.813	394	+4.536	374	+8.871
115	331	+1.076	331	+4.447	331	+9.337
116	374	+1.159	374	+4.724	206	+10.850
117	203	+4.825	333	+11.924	333	+17.236
118	333	+6.189	203	+17.959	203	+35.179
			Stockton			
1	287	-9.134	287	-16.939	287	-23.521
2	331	-6.955	331	-12.269	371	-16.479
3	371	-6.557	371	-12.009	331	-16.122
4	352	-5.949	354	-11.182	354	-15.890
5	354	-5.913	352	-11.083	352	-15.499
114	365	-0.522	365	-0.664	365	-0.516
115	206	-0.123	206	+2.272	206	+6.408
116	241	+2.241	241	+4.533	241	+6.824
117	394	+3.070	394	+6.082	394	+9.000
118	203	+14.485	203	+27.809	203	+40.068

Source: Simulated using estimated 1963 3-digit group base weights and variance-covariance matrix for 1958 through 1967.

104

Table 5.3 and Appendix Table A.5.2 offer further confirmation of the significant nonlinearity of the diversifying impact of alternative industries, and of substantial variability in the optimal diversifying industry across cities. None of the five "best" increments appears in the first five of all three cities. Several industries that are among the five "best" for one city are among the five "worst" for another. One industry group that is the "most-diversifying" for Detroit at the five percent level of increment is also the "least-diversifying" for Great Falls and Stockton at all levels of increment. That same industry falls from 1st to 114th for Detroit as Δ_k is raised from 5 to 15 percent. By this evidence there appears to be far less competition among regions for the most stable industries than was suggested by Thompson and Richardson at the outset. Furthermore, the magnitude of the range of potential diversifying impacts, from 9 percent improvement to 14 percent worsening in instability at the Δ_k = 5 percent level and from 23 percent improvement to 43 percent worsening at the Δ_k = 15 percent level for Stockton, for example, suggest greater potential influence, both positive and negative, from attention (or inattention) to the diversifying impact of industrial growth than is suggested by the overall tone of the existing literature on the subject.

Comparison of Table 5.2 and Table 5.3 reveals that at Δ_k = 5 percent none of the five "most-diversifying" industries according to the simulation results consist of the five "least-variable" industries. In only two cases is one of the five "least-diversifying" industries also one of the "most-variable." Similar results characterize a comparison of the Δ_k = 10 percent and the Δ_k = 15 percent cases, though not quite so clearly. At the same time there are several examples of "most-variable" industries that occur among the "most-diversifying" for one region or another.

A more systematic approach to this comparison of the optimal diversifying increments may be accomplished through rank correlation among the major variables. The Spearman rank correlation coefficients between the indices of instability for each industry and the simulated effects of increments in each industry are given in Table 5.4.

TABLE 5.4

Rank Correlation between Industry Variability
and Simulated Diversifying Impacts

	Δ_k = 5%	Δ_k = 10%	Δ_k = 15%
Detroit	-.5419	-.5909	-.6835
Great Falls	-.5805	-.6809	-.7578
Stockton	-.2612	-.3023	-.3558

These generally low and varying overall correlations offer further confirmation, in the opinion of the author, of the inadvisability of seeking diversifying industries on the basis of single-industry variability.

The Programming Approach

The third suggested strategy, determining optimally diversifying industrial increments by means of quadratic programming approach, offered the theoretical advantage of incorporating the nonlinearities over Δ_k and the multiplicity of alternative increments among a multitude of potential industries into a single maximizing problem. Given the choice of simple employment as the returns criterion in this case, the programming problem reduces here to the minimization of the portfolio variance (the squared index of instability) without variation in the expected returns across employment in various industries. This is formally equivalent to setting μ_j in (2.44) equal to one for all j.

In terms of Markowitz-Tobin portfolio analysis, the optimization undertaken here may be graphed as in Figure 5.1. The straightforward minimization of portfolio variance as an appropriate technique implies a linear "efficiency frontier" perpendicular to the expected returns axis. Choice of diversifying increments to existing industrial structure represents an attempt to move from an initial point such as A to points of greater employment and reduced variability, such as B, C, or D. The extent to which variability can be reduced is determined by the variance-covariance matrix, the magnitude of the increments, and the constraints upon treatment of preexisting industries.

In the empirical analysis undertaken here, for the sake of simplicity all current industry was constrained to levels greater than or equal to current levels, and all industries were assumed perfectly divisible in terms of feasible plant sizes. A total supply constraint was imposed by setting Δ in constraint (5.3c) equal to 5, 10, and 15 percent on each of three separate runs for each city.

This minimization problem was solved using the (118 × 118) national variance-covariance matrix, the (1 × 118) vectors of preexisting industry weights for each city, and a single total supply equality constraint with a gradient projection algorithm written by Donald Goldfarb [16]. The output of the minimization is in the form of a vector of $\hat{w}_j$ which minimize the portfolio variance subject to the 118 lower bounds (and implicit nonnegativity conditions) and the total supply equality. For purposes of comparison with the other approaches above, the following index of optimal increment was created:

$$(5.4) \qquad P_{j\Delta} = \frac{\hat{w}_j - w_j}{\Delta}.$$

106

FIGURE 5.1

The Implicit Diversification Strategy
Embodied in the Programming Approach

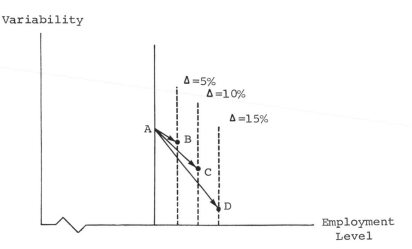

That is, the index expresses the increase in resources allocated
to industry j as a percent of the total increase in allocable resources.
The industries that were allocated the greatest percentages of the total
increment for each of the regions and under each of 5, 10, and 15 percent total increments are noted in Table 5.5, along with the minimum
index of instability achievable on each run within the given constraints.
The complete list of prior industry weights and ranked percentage distribution of increments among industries is given in Appendix Table A.5.4.

Not surprisingly we find in Table 5.5 that the programming approach
produces a ranked set of increments that corresponds fairly closely to
that dictated by the simulation approach. It also produces greater
reduction in the index of instability in every region, for every value of
Δ, than the best of the simulated single-industry increments.

Comparison of Tables 5.2 and 5.5 confirm the conclusions of the
earlier comparison of Tables 5.2 and 5.3. There is only slight correspondence apparent between those industries that are programmed for
the largest increments in the optimal vector of increments and the
"least-variable" industries.

Rank correlation coefficients in Tables 5.6 and 5.7 support both
the differences between the ranked single-industry variability and the
optimal vector of industry increments and the similarities between the
simulated and the programmed industry ranks as diversifying increments.

TABLE 5.5

Diversification According to Strategy 3:
Programming Minimization of Variability
(ranked optimally diversifying industry increments)

Rank	Δ = 5% Industry Group	Percent of Δ	Δ = 10% Industry Group	Percent of Δ	Δ = 15% Industry Group	Percent of Δ
			Detroit			
1	203	.125643	203	.100171	203	.083552
2	190	.083215	190	.070244	190	.062495
3	204	.043795	204	.040624	204	.037836
4	202	.038633	202	.036436	205	.034524
5	205	.037801	205	.036289	202	.034307
(Percentage change in variability	-10.631		-16.611		-18.882)	
			Great Falls			
1	206	.124064	190	.417428	205	.071876
2	190	.107007	301	.210430	190	.069622
3	366	.053216	206	.157166	366	.037017
4	301	.048256	387	.126193	301	.035216
5	272	.038857	205	.042791	272	.031187
(Percentage change in variability	-17.263		-21.118		.22.217)	
			Stockton			
1	287	831648	287	681614	287	667876
2	331	175892	331	212871	331	210029
3	312	001856	371	107365	371	128363
4	348	001765	321	000971	343	000650
5	324	001750	272	000969	327	000644
(Percentage change in variability	-12.333		-19.681		-27.197)	

Source: Calculated by the author.

TABLE 5.6

Rank Correlations between Industry Variability and Optimal Programmed Industry Increments

	$\Delta = 5\%$	$\Delta = 10\%$	$\Delta = 15\%$
Detroit	-.3404	-.3427	-.3494
Great Falls	-.2826	-.3410	-.4222
Stockton	-.0028	-.0142	-.0663

TABLE 5.7

Rank Correlations between Simulated Diversifying Impacts and Optimal Diversifying Increments

	$\Delta = 5\%$	$\Delta = 10\%$	$\Delta = 15\%$
Detroit	.7775	.7663	.7413
Great Falls	.7835	.7834	.7836
Stockton	.7552	.7899	.8672

The combined effects of interindustry interdependencies and pre-existing industrial structures do, indeed, appear to make a significant difference in the choice of diversifying industries. The variation in impacts among industries and across cities cannot be explained in any other way.

The absolute magnitude of the potential reduction in unemployment (or undersupply) also appears to warrant attention: the 5 percent probability unemployment rate would be reduced in Detroit, Great Falls and Stockton by 17.4, 28.5, and 20.2 percent respectively by means of the $\Delta = 5$ percent diversifying increments prescribed by the programming approach. Greater reductions would be possible with greater total increments. The relative effectiveness of the alternative strategies, given the measurement criterion, lends far greater credence to the simulation and programming approaches than to more traditional selection of relatively stable industries. The assumptions implicit in the present formulation of the programming solution and the cumbersome data requirements of a more realistic discrete programming variant diminish the superiority of the programming approach that would be suggested by the superior reductions in theoretical instability.

Further qualifications of these conclusions are also in order. The unweighted minimization of portfolio variance undertaken here has produced a vector of optimal diversifying increments that is unlikely to be identical to the optimal vector under more realistic weighted mini-mization. That is, rather than assume $\mu_j = 1$ for all j, individual indus-tries are likely to be preferred on the basis of relative rates of growth, relative wage levels, and other such characteristics of alternative returns criteria. More importantly, the fact that an industry appears to be the optimal diversifying increment for a region in this analysis, which ignores variation across regions in production costs, does not mean that the industry so-identified will be optimal when necessary location subsidies are incorporated in the analysis. Incorporation of such factors may require a prescreening or a postscreening of industries to reduce the feasibility set or the identified set to those industries that correspond to the spatial comparative advantage of a region. A more satisfying technical approach would consist of obtaining "bids" from each industry, as suggested in Chapter 4, with respect to the mag-nitude of the subsidy necessary to induce location of plants of each appropriate scale in the region of concern. These theoretical subsidy costs could then be incorporated directly into the optimization proce-dure. There is no reason to believe, however, that the incorporation of these additional costs will alter the results reported here in terms of the theoretical and empirical significance of considerations of regional industrial diversification.

6

OVERVIEW AND SUMMARY
OF CONCLUSIONS

The objective that we set ourselves at the outset of this study was the analysis of regional industrial diversification in the interest of developing both a greater understanding of the determinants of relative regional fluctuations in economic activity and in terms of clarifying conceptually the relationship between diversification and those fluctuations and evaluating at the same time alternative measures of industrial diversification.

In Chapter 1 it was developed that the full relationship between the industrial structure of a region and the historical variability of economic activity in that region has not been analyzed as thoroughly as would be required to justify the pessimism prevalent among leading regional economists with respect to the significance of such structure. That work still remains to be done. It was also noted in the initial chapter that one subset of that area of analysis, the analysis of relative diversification in regional industrial structures, had been hampered similarly by conceptual and practical problems that are likely to have resulted in understatement of the potential of diversification for reducing fluctuations in regional economic activity. It was to this more restricted problem that the theoretical and empirical work of this study was directed.

The four prior measures of industrial diversification specifically noted, the "ogive" measure, the "national average" measure, the "percent in durable goods," and the "minimum requirements" measure, were shown to be conceptually weak. The first two implied that some national average or "balance" of industries was conceptually equivalent to diversification, the third implied that all durable goods were perfectly correlated and more volatile than all nondurable goods, and the last implied that all regions should possess a given amount of all industry, ignoring the fact that such is true only for industries with market areas no larger than the smallest of the relevant regions.

In Chapter 2 a reformulation of the concept of regional diversification was offered. The reformulation of the concept took the tools of financial analysis of investment under conditions of risk and applied them to the problem of choosing industrial structures for regions where such choice was viewed as a process of investing real regional resources in economic activities, the precise returns from which cannot be known with certainty. Diversification in this context was specified as the process of choosing such industrial assets in a manner that minimized the variability associated with a given level of returns. The trade-off between rates of return on regional resources and variability in those rates was noted and it was demonstrated that the optimally diversified industrial structure was also the optimally specialized structure in that it produced an equating of the marginal rate of transformation of return into risk, along the frontier of most efficient combinations, with the marginal rate of substitution of risk for return along the specific region's assumed risk-return indifference surface.

This formulation of the diversification problem was shown to be consistent with traditional spatial equilibrium formulations for the determinate case. It was shown that so long as regional and national objectives are identical, the optimally diversified regional structure is also consistent with optimal national diversification. It was noted that the formulation could be made more realistic than first specified by incorporating preexisting industries, varying technology, economies of scale, and some forms of external economies. It was noted that individual regions could diversify to levels of fluctuations lower than those of the nation as a whole and that such regional diversification could reduce national fluctuations.

The formulation of the problem also yielded a measure of relative diversification, the relative portfolio variance, which appeared to offer improvements in conceptual basis over the alternative measures previously discussed.

The empirical analysis of fluctuation in manufacturing employment in 52 U.S. metropolitan regions offered an opportunity to test a number of hypotheses with respect to relative diversification. It was demonstrated that three of the earlier measures of industrial diversification were biases toward one or more structural characteristics of the sample regions, reducing thereby their usefulness for evaluating the significance of diversification of industrial structure in reducing observed fluctuations in manufacturing employment. It was similarly demonstrated that the most important variants of the portfolio variances were not biased.

It was demonstrated that the portfolio variances are highly significantly related to indices of observed instability and that none of the other measures are more than slightly related. The proportion of the variation in observed instability "explained" by the diversification of industrial structure as measured by the portfolio variance for the a priori most important case exceeded 42 percent. It appears unlikely that any other single varible would explain a larger proportion of that variability, and on that basis the significance of diversification of industrial structure as a policy for reducing such fluctuation may be considered strengthened.

112

A series of ancillary hypothesis tests produced additional information about the relationship between fluctuations and other structural characteristics of the sample of regions. It was found that there is little or no relationship between fluctuations and growth rates of the various regions. Similarly, contrary to the hypothesis advanced elsewhere that larger cities would be more stable cities, there was no significant relationship between size and fluctuation for the cities in this sample. In this latter case, however, it may be argued that the average size of cities in the sample was too large for the appearance of the expected diversification and that the diversification concomitant with greater size is manifest primarily among smaller cities.

Regional variations in rates of fluctuation and variation in diversification were found to be significant for both the Northeastern and the Western sections of the country. In the former area fluctuations were significantly less than in the rest of the nation; in the latter they were greater, over and above that which was explained by relative industrial diversification.

In Chapter 4 and important conceptual problem was briefly touched. A largely intuitive approach to spatial equilibrium of the labor force under uncertainty with respect to employment fluctuations led to the tentative conclusions that regional competitiveness in terms of nominal wages for constant quality labor could be affected by relative diversification and that market location processes might not lead to the full internalization of stabilizing or destabilizing external effects of expanding existing plants or locating new plants within a region. Optimal diversification, whether viewed from local or national perspectives, does not appear to be a likely result of laissez faire location decisions.

A number of relatively pragmatic, policy-related concerns with respect to the stabilizing potential of diversification policy were explored in Chapter 5. By means of a series of simulations of the potential diversifying effects of alternative increments of each of a broad set of industries, it was possible to generate initial support for three ideas. First, it does not appear likely that the traditional diversification approach, seeking nationally stable industries, will lead to the greatest diversifying effect in most cases. The optimally diversifying set of industry increments is seen to be a complex but tractable function of prior industrial structure, size of contemplated increments, and interindustry relationships. Second, the absolute magnitude of simulated reductions in fluctuation-related unemployment was shown to be such that attention to such policy may prove more warranted than previously appeared to be the case. Finally, it appears to be possible to estimate, in rough terms, the potential diversifying or stabilizing effect of any given increment to a regional industrial structure. Such an ability would appear to be crucial to the adoption of a policy of diversification-oriented subsidies, lest the subsidies offered exceed conceivable benefits.

The treatment of the diversification problem undertaken here retains may conceptual and empirical shortcomings. It has been a treatment that is partial and otherwise oversimplified in many ways. Some of the qualifications of the analysis have been raised in individual chapters; it will serve as well, I believe, to close by introducing further reservations.

It has been mentioned in several places above that diversification with respect to employment alone is seldom likely to be an actual goal. More complex criteria such as employment weighted by wages will be needed to move the analysis closer to realistic planning goals. On a broader level, diversification per se is seldom likely to be the single-minded objective of regional development policy. The goal of increasing stability must be viewed as merely a part of development policy that will also include growth of per capita income as a goal, perhaps the most heavily weighted goal. Targets with respect to income distribution, environmental quality, size per se, or alleviation of specific local problems are also candidates for inclusion in the multiple-criteria policy-planning framework, along with diversification. To treat diversification as a separable phenomenon is to understate the complexity of the problem.

Even as a separable problem, diversification is unlikely to result from a single-shot one-time analysis of the problem as may appear to be implicit in the techniques used here. All changes in the industrial structure will effect the distribution of optimally diversifying increments. The problem requires a more dynamic approach to programming a solution, perhaps an approach such as the adaptive optimization possible through optimal control theory.

The full significance of the industrial structure varible for relative regional economic behavior remains to be explored. The analysis here, for example, has included consideration of interindustry relations within regions in indirect fashion, through interindustry covariances that were assumed identical nationwide. Specific direct evaluation of those interindustry relations, especially in terms of their mitigating or exacerbating effects upon the reception of exogenous shocks, needs to be studied using input-output analyses for measuring production interdependence and the calculation of elasticities for consumption interdependence.

No attempt was made to test whether diversification as specified here would, in fact, tend to lead to a reduction in national aggregate fluctuations. That, as well as other aspects of the theoretical model that are mentioned above, require new data sets and different testing procedures.

Finally, the assumption that interindustry covariances are uniform nationwide begs for testing. That is, we believe, the most heroic assumption made in the empirical analysis given the a priori reasons why such is unlikely. Estimation of regional interindustry covariances for much smaller regions will be necessary to test the sensitivity of the conclusions here presented, to increase the explanatory significance of industrial structure (if such is possible), and, ultimately, to make the analysis outlined here as useful as possible for individual regional planners who seek to diversify their industrial structures in significant and efficient ways.

ON THE USE OF MEAN-VARIANCE ANALYSIS IN THIS STUDY

The utility function assumed for individual regions, as specified in equation (2.17), contains as arguments both the expected return and the variance of that return, introduced directly. This form for introducing consideration of risk is eminently convenient, permitting both the straightforward utilization of programming techniques for the derivation of optimal industrial structes and the use of mathematically tractable estimates of the relative attractiveness of individual portfolios. Given the extensive recent criticism of the utility theory implicit in the specification, it is also potentially hazardous. In the following paragraphs we shall consider the major criticisms that have been advanced, the replies offered to date, and the qualifications that must consequently be introduced, on utility theory grounds, for any conclusions derived from this specification.

The criticism has taken three forms: (1) questioning of the applicability and precise meaning of utility functions that introduce directly a measure of risk; (2) questioning of the appropriateness of considering only the mean and variance of any given utility function for wealth or, in general, for returns from a stochastic process; and (3) criticism of the use of the variance as a specific measure of the "riskiness" of a stochastic process. The first criticism is that which has been developed least. Hanoch and Levy noted in a footnote to a recent article [20, p. 342] that the logical basis for direct introduction of risk seems to be questionable "or at least vague." Markowitz [33] and Sharpe [51] have defended the specification as merely a useful means of referring to utility analysis, which is dependent solely upon the mean and variance of the probability distribution on returns.

It is this latter assumption that has been subjected to the greatest barrage of criticism. Markowitz initially claimed that consideration of only the first two moments of the distribution could be justified because the third moment, the measure of skewness for a normal distribution, is associated with a propensity to gamble. That is, he suggested [32, pp. 90-91], a utility maximizing investor would never accept an actuarially fair bet unless the distribution on returns were skewed toward positive returns. Tsiang, however, has noted that a preference for such skewness, requiring knowledge of the third moment, is in general a logical feature of an expected utility maximizer with decreasing or constant absolute risk aversion with respect to possible increases in wealth [62, pp. 10-11].

Tobin noted in his classic treatment of risk, which used only two moments, that such could be justified when the investor's utility function for wealth was quadratic (and constrained to the range of increasing marginal utility of wealth) or where the relevant subjective probability distribution on returns from various investments were multivariate normal or characterized by other two-moment distributions [60, p. 77]. Numerous objectionable characteristics of quadratic utility functions were quickly noted by Hicks [21], Richter [44], Lintner [28, 29], Pratt [41], and Arrow [1].

The criticisms of Pratt and Arrow were the most telling, for they denied to quadratic utility functions, throughout their range, an intuitively essential property: decreasing absolute risk aversion. As defined by Arrow, decreasing absolute risk aversion "amounts to saying that the willingness to engage in small bets of fixed size increases with wealth, in the sense that the odds demanded diminish" [1, p 96]. For quadratic utility functions, as wealth increases toward the implicit level of maximum utility (that is, where $du/dy = 0$), absolute risk aversion actually increases, moving toward infinity and indicating that the willingness to gamble for a bet of fixed size will tend to disappear.

The alternative assumption of multivariate normality has appeared to be even less plausible since it rules out asymmetry or skewness in the distribution on returns and because returns from investments are more likely to be distributed lognormally than normally. Cootner [9], for example, has established this last point with respect to investment in financial securities based on the reasoning that the accumulated exponential returns on investments are the products rather than the sums of random factors aggregated over time.

Finally, Feldstein [12] has shown that the lognormal distribution, which is a two-parameter distribution as defined by Tobin, produces results consistent with mean-variance analysis only over a limited range. Tobin [59, p. 13] subsequently noted that the normal distribution is the only two-parameter distribution for which mean-variance analysis is adequate.

As though such fundamental criticism were insufficient, the variance itself has come under increasing attack as a measure of relative riskiness. Markowitz himself noted that the variance could be considered unrealistic in that it weighted positive fluctuations (returns above the mean). He suggested, as an alternative, the use of the semivariance, the mean of squared negative fluctuations [33, p. 187].

Recent criticism has been somewhat more abstract. The basic question relates to the conditions under which one probability distribution on returns will "dominate" another. This stochastic dominance of one random variable, say x, over another, say y, was defined by Hanoch and Levy [20, p. 336] as meaning that the expected utility of x is greater than or equal to that of y for every utility function in the class of admissible utility functions and positive for at least one. They conclude:

116

The identification of riskiness with variance, or with any other single measure of dispersion is clearly unsound. There are many obvious cases, where more dispersion is desirable, if it is accompanied by an upward shift in the location of the distribution, or by an increasing positive asymmetry [20, p. 344].

A more general analysis of the relationship between increasing risk and the variance as a measure of that risk has been provided recently by Rothschild and Stiglitz [46, 47]. They incorporate directly the possibility of asymmetry in the distribution on returns through a measure of "mean preserving spread." Using indefinite integrals of differences of cumulative distribution functions, they demonstrate that three alternative plausible definitions of "riskiness" produce a partial ordering of distribution functions different from that produced by the variance and "more consistent with the natural meaning of increasing risk" [46, p. 227].

As they themselves note, however, definitions of increasing risk are chosen for their usefulness as well as their consistency [46, p. 227]. Though elegant, their alternative approach is empirically virtually inoperable and conceptually very clumsy. In terms of diversification analysis, for example, they have been unable to establish a diversification theorem for any but the simplest case, that of identical independent distributions. Hadar and Russell [18], who have generalized the stochastic dominance analysis using cumulative distribution functions, have been able to handle the nonidentical but independent case, but they have not yet been able to deal with interdependence nor have they derived an empirically tractable alternative to the variance.

Can any justification for mean-variance analysis other than operational usefulness be offered? One defense that may be particularly appropriate to the present framework is that suggested by Roy [48]. He has shown that investors who follow a strategy that minimizes the upper bound of the probability that the realized outcome will fall below a preassigned "disaster level" should maximize the ratio of the excess expected portfolio return (over the disaster level) to the standard deviation of the return on the portfolio. His conclusion, dubbed "safety-first," depends on neither the form of the utility function nor upon multivariate normality on returns. This approach appears reasonable in the context of regional planning. For "disaster" may be defined in terms of unemployment above a certain level, income below a given level, or negative changes in income or employment of more than a given percentage per unit of time.

Feldstein suggested, alternatively, that

an acceptable assumption is that the investor make the statistical mistake of assuming that all distributions are stable, i.e., of assuming that the portfolio has the same two-parameter distribution as its constituents. Although such an assumption is

117

a "statistical mistake" unless the assets are normally distributed (or have infinite variance), it corresponds to the implicit assumption that underlies all current mean-variance portfolio analysis. In addition to the plausibility, it has the virtue of allowing the investor to act according to Von Neumann-Morgenstern axioms of expected utility maximization—although using incorrect and mutually inconsistent subjective probability distributions. [12, p. 10]

Two potentially more significant bases for resurrecting mean-variance analysis from theoretical near-oblivion have been suggested by Samuelson [49] and Tsiang [62]. Samuelson, writing first, noted that by considering utility functions in terms of their corresponding Taylor's series, the third and higher moments of such functions could be ignored in those cases where the risk involved was absolutely very small.

Tsiang has made an important addition to that analysis by noting that if the convergence of the series is "sufficiently fast" the terms beyond the second moment can be neglected. "Then, indeed," he suggests, "the expected utility can be approximately determined by the first two moments, mean and variance, even if the utility function is not quadratic, nor . . . the uncertain outcomes normally distributed" [62, p. 13].

Using negative exponential and CES utility functions (for which the Pratt-Arrow properties hold), he then demonstrates that the speed of convergence is inversely related to the magnitude of the relative risk involved. That is, "there is a justification for the use of [mean-variance] analysis . . . provided the aggregate risk taken by the individual concerned is small compared with his total wealth."

For a lognormal utility function, furthermore, he notes that Feldstein's conclusions concur with his. Mean variance analysis produces the desired concavity of indifference curves so long as the coefficient of variation of returns is less than $\sqrt{0.5} = .7071$. In the empirical analysis in this study the coefficient of variation of returns on manufacturing employment in 52 U.S. metropolitan areas never exceeded .22, and the mean (of the principal series) is less than .03.

For purposes of this study, therefore, mean-variance analysis is used primarily because of its operational convenience. It is used further with some confidence that the convergence of the Taylor expansion of any appropriate utility function will be relatively fast, reducing the significance of the third and higher moments. As Tobin has noted with respect to his own analysis, however, extension of the analysis of regional industrial structure from one moment to two moments is not offered as "the complete job or the final word" [59, p. 14]. Rather, it is hoped that this relatively simple extension of determinate analysis will provide sufficient benefit in terms of improved insight and operational usefulness to offset the forced simplification and virtual approximation inherent in the mean-variance approach.

TABLE A. 3. 1

Geographical Compositions of Sample
Metropolitan Regions, with Full Titles

SMSA Complete Title	Component Counties
Albany-Schenectady-Troy, NY	Albany
	Rensselaer
	Saratoga
	Schenectady
Albuquerque, NM	Bernalillo
Allentown-Bethlehem-Easton, PA-NJ	Lehigh County, PA
	Northampton, PA
	Warren, NJ
Atlanta, GA	Clayton
	Cobb
	DeKalb
	Fulton
	Gwinnett
Baltimore, MD	Baltimore City
	Anne Arundel
	Baltimore
	Carroll
	Harford
	Howard
Baton Rouge, LA	East Baton Rouge
Binghamton, NY-PA	Broome County, NY
	Tioga County, NY
	Susquehanna County, PA
Buffalo, NY	Erie
	Niagara
Chattanooga, TN-GA	Hamilton County, TN
	Walker County, GA

(continued)

SMSA Complete Title	Component Counties
Chicago, IL	Cook
	Du Page
	Kane
	Lake
	McHenry
	Will
Dallas, TX	Collin
	Dallas
	Denton
	Ellis
	Kaufman
	Rockwall
Denver, CO	Adams
	Arapahoe
	Boulder
	Denver
	Jefferson
Detroit, MI	Macomb
	Oakland
	Wayne
Erie, PA	Erie
Fort Wayne, IN	Allen
Fresno, CA	Fresno
Gary-Hammond-East Chicago, IN	Lake
	Porter
Great Falls, MT	Cascade
Greensboro-Highpoint, NC	Guilford
Indianapolis, IN	Boone
	Hamilton
	Hancock
	Hendricks
	Johnson
	Marion
	Morgan
	Shelby
Knoxville, TN	Anderson
	Blount
	Knox

SMSA Complete Title	Component Counties
Lancaster, PA	Lancaster
Los Angeles-Long Beach, CA	Los Angeles
Miami, FL	Dade
Minneapolis-St. Paul, MN	Anoka
	Dakota
	Hennepin
	Ramsey
	Washington
New York, NY	Bronx
	Kings
	Nassau
	New York
	Queens
	Richmond
	Rockland
	Suffolk
	Westchester
Omaha-Council Bluffs, NB-IA	Douglas County, NB
	Sarpy County, NB
	Pottawattamie County, IA
Philadelphia, PA-NJ	Bucks County, PA
	Chester County, PA
	Delaware County, PA
	Montgomery County, PA
	Philadelphia, County, PA
	Burlington County, NJ
	Camden County, NJ
	Gloucester County, NJ
Phoenix AZ	Maricopa
Pittsburgh, PA	Allegheny
	Beaver
	Washington
	Westmoreland
Portland, OR-WA	Clackamas County, OR
	Multnomah County, OR
	Washington County, OR
	Clark County, WA
Racine, WI	Racine

(continued)

121

SMSA Complete Title	Component Counties
Reading, PA	Berks
Rochester, NY	Livingston
	Monroe
	Orleans
	Wayne
Salt Lake City, UT	Davis
	Salt Lake County
San Diego, CA	San Diego
San Francisco-Oakland, CA	Alameda
	Contra Costa
	Marin
	San Francisco
	San Mateo
San Jose, CA	Santa Clara
Savannah, GA	Chatham
Seattle-Everett, WA	King
	Snohomish
Sioux Falls, SD	Minnehaha
Spokane, WA	Spokane
Stockton, CA	San Joaquin
Syracuse, NY	Madison
	Onondaga
	Oswego
Tacoma, WA	Pierce
Tampa-St. Petersburg, FL	Hillsborough
	Pinellas
Topeka, KA	Shawnee
Trenton, NJ	Mercer
Tucson, AZ	Pima
Utica-Rome, NY	Herkimer
	Oneida
Wilkes-Barre-Hazleton, PA	Luzerne
Winston-Salem, NC	Forsyth

Source: Standard Metropolitan Statistical Areas, 1967 (Washington, D.C.: Government Printing Office, 1967).

118 Combined Industry Groups
and 3-Digit SIC Equivalents

Combined Industry Group	SIC Equivalents	Description
19	191, 192, 193, and 194	Ordnance and accessories
201	201	Meat products
202	202	Dairy products
203	203	Canned, cured, and frozen foods
204	204	Grain mill products
205	205	Bakery products
206	206	Sugar
207	207	Confectionary and related products
208	208	Beverages
209	209	Miscellaneous foods and kindred products
211	211	Cigarettes
212	212	Cigars
221	221	Weaving mills, cotton
222	222	Weaving mills, synthetics
223	223	Weaving and finishing mills, wool
224	224	Narrow fabric mills
225	225	Knitting mills
226	226	Textile finishing, except wool
227	227	Floor covering mills
228	228	Yarn and thread mills
229	229	Miscellaneous textile goods
231	231	Men's and boys' suits and coats
232	232	Men's and boys' furnishings
233	233	Women's and misses' outerwear
234	234	Women's and children's undergarments
235	235	Hats, caps, and millinery
236	236	Children's outerwear
237	237, 238	Fur goods and miscellaneous apparel
239	239	Miscellaneous fabricated textile products
241	241	Logging camps and logging contractors
242	242	Sawmills and planing mills
243	243	Millwork, plywood, and related products
244	244	Wooden containers
249	249	Miscellaneous wood products

(continued)

Combined Industry Group	SIC Equivalents	Description
251	251	Household furniture
252	252	Office furniture
253	253, 259	Other furniture and fixtures
254	254	Partitions and fixtures
261	261, 262, 266	Paper and pulp mills
263	263	Paperboard mills
264	264	Miscellaneous converted paper products
265	265	Paperboard containers and boxes
271	271	Newspapers
272	272	Periodicals
273	273	Books
274	274, 276, 277, and 279	Miscellaneous publishing
275	275	Commercial printing
281	281	Industrial chemicals
282	282	Plastics materials and synthetics
283	283	Drugs
284	284	Soap, cleaners, and toilet goods
285	285	Paints and allied products
286	286, 289	Other chemical products
287	287	Agricultural chemicals
291	291	Petroleum refining
295	295. 299	Other petroleum and coal products
301	301	Tires and inner tubes
302	302, 303, 306	Other rubber products
307	307	Miscellaneous plastics products
311	311	Leather tanning and finishing
312	312, 313, 315 317, and 319	Other leather products
314	314	Footwear, except rubber
321	321	Flat glass
322	322	Glass and glassware, pressed or blown
324	324	Cement, hydraulic
325	325	Structural clay products
326	326	Pottery and related products
327	327	Concrete, gypsum, and plaster products
328	328, 329	Other stone and nonmetallic mineral products

Combined Industry Group	SIC Equivalents	Description
331	331	Blast furnace and basic steel products
332	332	Iron and steel foundaries
333	333, 334	Nonferrous metals
335	335	Nonferrous rolling and drawing
336	336	Nonferrous foundaries
339	339	Miscellaneous primary metal products
341	341	Metal cans
342	342	Cutlery, hand tools, and hardware
343	343	Plumbing and heating, except electric
344	344	Fabricated structural metal products
345	345	Screw machine products, bolts, etc.
346	346	Metal stampings
347	347	Metal services, not elsewhere classified
348	348	Miscellaneous fabricated wire products
349	349	Miscellaneous fabricated metal products
351	351	Engines and turbines
352	352	Farm machinery
353	353	Construction and related machinery
354	354	Metal working machinery
355	355	Special industry machinery
356	356	General industrial machinery
357	357	Office and computing machines
358	358	Service industry machines
359	359	Miscellaneous machinery, except electric
361	361	Electric test and distributing equipment
362	362	Electrical industrial apparatus
363	363	Household appliances
364	364	Electric lighting and wiring equipment
365	365	Radio and TV receiving equipment
366	366	Communication equipment
367	367	Electronic components and accessories
369	369	Misc. electrical equipment and supplies
371	371	Motor vehicles and equipment
372	372	Aircraft and parts
373	373	Ship and boat building and repairing
374	374	Railroad equipment
375	375, 385	Other transportation equipment

(continued)

Combined Industry Group	SIC Equivalents	Description
381	381	Engineering and scientific instruments
382	382	Mechanical measuring and control devices
383	383, 385	Optical and ophthalmic goods
384	384	Medical instruments and supplies
386	386	Photographic equipment and supplies
387	387	Watches, clocks, and watchcases
391	391	Jewelry, silverware, and plated wire
394	394	Toys and sporting goods
395	395	Pens, pencils, office, and art supplies
396	396	Costume jewelry and notions
393	393	Other manufacturing industries

Source: Employment and Earnings, United States, 1909-1968 (Washington, D. C.: Government Printing Office, 1970).

118 Industry Groups:
Empirical Indices of Instability
(column ranks in parentheses)

Combined Industry Group	Unadjusted		Detrended		Detrended and Deseasonalized	
19	.17427	(9)	.10417	(7)	.10863	(2)
201	.02564	(115)	.02298	(97)	.01258	(111)
202	.06103	(89)	.02533	(89)	.00732	(118)
203	.24180	(3)	.23755	(1)	.05418	(21)
204	.02605	(114)	.02358	(95)	.01337	(108)
205	.02668	(113)	.01169	(118)	.00793	(117)
206	.20898	(5)	.20750	(2)	.05793	(16)
207	.07246	(79)	.06587	(17)	.01737	(102)
208	.04875	(97)	.03474	(67)	.01411	(106)
209	.02131	(117)	.02053	(102)	.01100	(113)
211	.04201	(104)	.02320	(96)	.02211	(88)
212	.13318	(21)	.05849	(24)	.05807	(15)
221	.05363	(95)	.02497	(91)	.02517	(78)
222	.08335	(67)	.01995	(104)	.01976	(96)
223	.11655	(34)	.04762	(40)	.04394	(33)
224	.05364	(94)	.03056	(77)	.03087	(67)
225	.04874	(98)	.03670	(63)	.02799	(73)
226	.02462	(116)	.01845	(108)	.01882	(98)
227	.09251	(56)	.03686	(61)	.03115	(65)
228	.05298	(96)	.02559	(88)	.02604	(77)
229	.06193	(87)	.03698	(60)	.03757	(51)
231	.04212	(103)	.02723	(86)	.02381	(80)
232	.10092	(44)	.03939	(56)	.03806	(47)
233	.06402	(86)	.02965	(81)	.02188	(90)
234	.04366	(101)	.03071	(76)	.02241	(87)
235	.14369	(16)	.07904	(16)	.04220	(38)
236	.03336	(110)	.02796	(85)	.01795	(100)
237	.07453	(77)	.04953	(38)	.02689	(76)
239	.09965	(46)	.03100	(75)	.02244	(86)
241	.10890	(42)	.10606	(5)	.05126	(27)
242	.08627	(63)	.05014	(36)	.04087	(40)
243	.06911	(81)	.05374	(33)	.05001	(29)
244	.08880	(61)	.03840	(58)	.03269	(58)
249	.13584	(20)	.02799	(84)	.02747	(74)

(continued)

Combined Industry Group	Unadjusted		Detrended		Detrended and Deseasonalized	
251	.08205	(69)	.03260	(70)	.03208	(61)
252	.12271	(27)	.03922	(57)	.03963	(43)
253	.09593	(49)	.04453	(42)	.04346	(35)
254	.09803	(47)	.03991	(54)	.03668	(52)
261	.02204	(118)	.01971	(105)	.01777	(101)
263	.03715	(109)	.01905	(107)	.01946	(97)
264	.12696	(25)	.01623	(113)	.01574	(104)
265	.08192	(70)	.01652	(112)	.01281	(110)
271	.04242	(102)	.01346	(115)	.01308	(109)
272	.02965	(111)	.02215	(100)	.02058	(93)
273	.11605	(36)	.02257	(98)	.02301	(84)
274	.09078	(58)	.01309	(116)	.01091	(114)
275	.05368	(93)	.01178	(117)	.01070	(116)
278	.07880	(74)	.02659	(87)	.02451	(79)
281	.04021	(107)	.01444	(114)	.01385	(107)
282	.12859	(24)	.02218	(99)	.02255	(85)
283	.08393	(66)	.02009	(103)	.01985	(95)
284	.08910	(60)	.01829	(109)	.01082	(115)
285	.04112	(106)	.01966	(106)	.01250	(112)
286	.11933	(30)	.05930	(22)	.06094	(12)
287	.12180	(28)	.09632	(8)	.01649	(103)
291	.09460	(52)	.01685	(111)	.01555	(105)
295	.05713	(92)	.05430	(31)	.02330	(82)
301	.06183	(88)	.05877	(23)	.05643	(18)
302	.07913	(73)	.03671	(62)	.03443	(54)
307	.28504	(2)	.03014	(79)	.02859	(71)
311	.06764	(83)	.02427	(93)	.02332	(81)
312	.04166	(105)	.04048	(52)	.02745	(75)
314	.02723	(112)	.02407	(94)	.02195	(89)
321	.09401	(53)	.09468	(9)	.09870	(4)
322	.07682	(76)	.02511	(90)	.02046	(94)
324	.08104	(71)	.04736	(41)	.02305	(83)
325	.06436	(84)	.04982	(37)	.03787	(49)
326	.04511	(99)	.03394	(69)	.03334	(55)
327	.09302	(55)	.06327	(20)	.03071	(68)
328	.05785	(91)	.02865	(83)	.02829	(72)

Combined Industry Group	Unadjusted		Detrended		Detrended and Deseasonalized	
331	.12085	(29)	.12069	(3)	.11764	(1)
332	.08741	(62)	.05090	(35)	.05239	(24)
333	.09392	(54)	.07963	(15)	.08023	(6)
335	.08017	(72)	.03636	(64)	.03792	(48)
336	.13953	(17)	.04172	(46)	.04267	(36)
339	.09683	(48)	.04102	(48)	.04224	(37)
341	.06425	(85)	.05951	(21)	.04432	(32)
342	.09490	(51)	.04078	(51)	.03777	(50)
343	.03813	(108)	.03173	(73)	.03157	(63)
344	.11840	(32)	.08196	(13)	.07815	(8)
345	.10970	(41)	.04353	(44)	.04499	(31)
346	.11349	(40)	.05512	(29)	.05172	(26)
347	.15402	(12)	.05424	(32)	.05342	(22)
348	.08439	(65)	.04104	(47)	.04188	(39)
349	.11429	(38)	.02126	(101)	.02185	(91)
351	.08308	(68)	.03259	(71)	.03305	(57)
352	.12327	(26)	.06366	(19)	.05432	(20)
353	.11842	(31)	.05470	(30)	.05549	(19)
354	.15013	(13)	.04079	(50)	.03852	(46)
355	.09249	(57)	.03170	(74)	.03191	(62)
356	.11762	(33)	.03193	(72)	.03324	(56)
357	.19677	(6)	.02992	(80)	.03115	(64)
358	.11554	(37)	.03466	(68)	.03212	(60)
359	.13860	(18)	.03744	(59)	.03891	(45)
361	.09060	(59)	.04234	(45)	.04393	(34)
362	.09984	(45)	.04849	(39)	.05062	(28)
363	.07158	(80)	.03950	(55)	.03896	(44)
364	.16895	(10)	.03554	(65)	.03633	(53)
365	.18197	(8)	.08822	(10)	.07505	(10)
366	.14461	(15)	.06428	(18)	.06704	(11)
367	.24019	(4)	.06985	(14)	.08344	(5)
369	.06846	(82)	.05842	(25)	.05821	(14)
371	.12908	(23)	.08669	(11)	.07546	(9)
372	.11646	(35)	.04424	(43)	.04600	(30)
373	.09496	(50)	.04080	(49)	.04031	(42)
374	.18272	(7)	.10535	(6)	.10681	(3)
375	.31611	(1)	.08624	(12)	.07833	(7)

(continued)

TABLE A. 3. 3 continued

Combined Industry Group	Unadjusted		Detrended		Detrended and Deseasonalized	
381	.07716	(75)	.05682	(27)	.05935	(13)
382	.08601	(64)	.05695	(26)	.05774	(17)
383	.10849	(43)	.03019	(78)	.03103	(66)
384	.13197	(22)	.01744	(110)	.01803	(99)
386	.15741	(11)	.02908	(82)	.02890	(70)
387	.11428	(39)	.05344	(34)	.05241	(23)
391	.07381	(78)	.03505	(66)	.02921	(69)
393	.14887	(14)	.05613	(28)	.05222	(25)
394	.13740	(19)	.11187	(4)	.04061	(41)
395	.05880	(90)	.02433	(92)	.02066	(92)
396	.04432	(100)	.04044	(53)	.03235	(59)

Source: Calculated by the author.

118 Industry Groups: Mean Percent of Employment
in Sample Regions and Mean National Employment Levels
(column ranks in parentheses)

Combined Industry Group	"National" Average Percent		Mean National Employment (1958-67)	
19	.02351	(7)	240. 350	(21)
201	.03220	(1)	319. 852	(9)
202	.02049	(12)	298. 123	(11)
203	.02161	(9)	254. 370	(18)
204	.00937	(37)	130. 370	(49)
205	.02517	(6)	292. 192	(12)
206	.00262	(90)	35. 897	(108)
207	.00545	(57)	78. 348	(73)
208	.10708	(16)	218. 491	(25)
209	.01035	(31)	142. 697	(47)
211	.00288	(81)	38. 152	(107)
212	.00370	(72)	25. 202	(117)
221	.00499	(60)	241. 977	(19)
222	.00138	(106)	87. 802	(68)
223	.00095	(114)	50. 581	(94)
224	.00088	(115)	28. 347	(116)
225	.01857	(14)	219. 802	(24)
226	.00223	(98)	76. 317	(77)
227	.00136	(107)	39. 036	(105)
228	.00309	(80)	106. 602	(59)
229	.00174	(105)	70. 749	(82)
231	.00774	(41)	118. 595	(55)
232	.01388	(23)	322. 902	(8)
233	.01923	(13)	391. 451	(5)
234	.00484	(61)	118. 905	(54)
235	.00099	(113)	31. 934	(112)
236	.00350	(75)	77. 092	(76)
237	.00248	(92)	73. 728	(80)
239	.00686	(49)	149. 640	(45)
241	.00228	(96)	85. 924	(70)
242	.00738	(46)	263. 284	(17)
243	.01170	(28)	154. 526	(43)
244	.00214	(99)	38. 180	(106)
249	.00326	(77)	67. 202	(87)

(continued)

Combined Industry Group	"National" Average Percent		Mean National Employment (1958-67)	
251	.01470	(22)	287.617	(14)
252	.00130	(108)	33.274	(110)
253	.00192	(102)	44.737	(98)
254	.00267	(88)	40.970	(103)
261	.00799	(40)	216.340	(27)
263	.00559	(56)	68.476	(86)
264	.00965	(35)	146.432	(46)
265	.01339	(25)	188.681	(30)
271	.03091	(2)	332.914	(7)
272	.00312	(79)	70.198	(85)
273	.00626	(53)	75.688	(78)
274	.00672	(50)	115.664	(56)
275	.02077	(11)	300.234	(10)
278	.00213	(100)	49.538	(96)
281	.01580	(18)	288.748	(13)
282	.00655	(51)	172.807	(34)
283	.00531	(59)	114.102	(57)
284	.00443	(65)	98.317	(64)
285	.00332	(76)	63.986	(88)
286	.00239	(95)	84.548	(71)
287	.00457	(63)	49.843	(95)
291	.00882	(38)	162.502	(38)
295	.00241	(94)	34.573	(109)
301	.00122	(109)	101.702	(63)
302	.01555	(20)	160.602	(40)
307	.00112	(111)	160.859	(39)
311	.00009	(118)	32.738	(111)
312	.10244	(26)	87.523	(69)
314	.00009	(117)	237.752	(22)
321	.00247	(93)	31.298	(114)
322	.00099	(112)	110.097	(58)
324	.00287	(82)	39.952	(104)
325	.00273	(85)	71.077	(81)
326	.00431	(68)	44.110	(101)
327	.01574	(19)	165.407	(37)
328	.00716	(48)	124.697	(52)

Combined Industry Group	"National" Average Percent	Mean National Employment (1958-67)
331	.02141 (10)	616.628 (3)
332	.01179 (27)	218.034 (26)
333	.01849 (15)	70.626 (83)
335	.01626 (17)	188.765 (29)
336	.00269 (87)	79.589 (72)
339	.00265 (89)	62.583 (89)
341	.00367 (74)	62.203 (90)
342	.00641 (52)	141.952 (48)
343	.00434 (67)	78.185 (74)
344	.02870 (4)	357.377 (6)
345	.00269 (86)	91.529 (66)
346	.00542 (58)	200.653 (28)
347	.00325 (78)	70.311 (84)
348	.00285 (84)	57.892 (91)
349	.00756 (43)	128.789 (50)
351	.00372 (71)	89.529 (67)
352	.00744 (45)	124.722 (51)
353	.00970 (33)	232.617 (23)
354	.01090 (30)	275.545 (15)
355	.00762 (42)	178.312 (32)
356	.01349 (24)	241.272 (20)
357	.00813 (39)	171.224 (35)
358	.00721 (47)	105.940 (60)
359	.00982 (32)	177.628 (33)
361	.00748 (44)	168.032 (36)
362	.01112 (29)	185.137 (31)
363	.00368 (73)	159.423 (41)
364	.00623 (54)	155.037 (42)
365	.00437 (66)	121.904 (53)
366	.03016 (3)	410.484 (4)
367	.01475 (21)	273.942 (16)
369	.00412 (70)	103.165 (62)
371	.02840 (5)	736.143 (1)
372	.02325 (8)	682.337 (2)
373	.00963 (36)	151.888 (44)
374	.00413 (69)	46.742 (97)
375	.00175 (104)	44.271 (100)

(continued)

Combined Industry Group	"National" Average Percent	Mean National Employment (1958-67)
381	. 00225 (97)	74. 128 (79)
382	. 00454 (64)	95. 644 (65)
383	. 00191 (103)	42. 744 (102)
384	. 00248 (91)	52. 624 (93)
386	. 00475 (62)	77. 822 (75)
387	. 00120 (110)	29. 799 (115)
391	. 00285 (83)	44. 373 (99)
393	. 00068 (116)	21. 701 (118)
394	. 00574 (55)	104. 476 (61)
395	. 00201 (101)	31. 792 (113)
396	. 00966 (34)	57. 533 (92)

Source: Calculated by the author.

TABLE A. 3. 5

Mean Regional Manufacturing Employment Levels, 1958-67,
and Employment in "Administrative and Auxiliary"

	Metropolitan Region	Mean Manufacturing Employment (1958-67)	"Administrative and Auxiliary" 1963 Employment	Percent of 1963 Manufacturing Employment
1	Albany	63.597	7930	11.2
2	Albuquerque	7.933	0	0.0
3	Allentown et al.	76.927	4697	5.7
4	Atlanta	96.790	2819	3.0
5	Baltimore	198.300	3646	2.1
6	Baton Rouge	16.906	106	0.8
7	Binghamton	45.452	1033	3.0
8	Buffalo	172.244	3655	2.3
9	Chattanooga	43.242	342	0.8
10	Chicago	883.114	60301	6.8
11	Dallas	112.949	3667	3.7
12	Denver	65.274	1977	3.2
13	Detroit	519.531	65202	14.4
14	Erie	37.812	588	1.5
15	Fort Wayne	37.209	1546	3.9
16	Fresno	14.686	48	0.3
17	Gary et al.	102.244	539	0.8
18	Great Falls	3.318	75	2.8
19	Greensboro et al.	45.781	4431	8.9
20	Indianapolis	118.047	2762	2.6
21	Knoxville	43.182	161	0.5
22	Lancaster	48.922	4072	7.7
23	Los Angeles et al.	761.147	23093	3.4
24	Miami	48.400	747	1.6
25	Minneapolis et al.	164.049	17349	10.5

(continued)

TABLE A. 3. 5 continued

	Metropolitan Region	Mean Manufacturing Employment (1958-67)	"Administrative and Auxiliary" 1963 Employment	Percent of 1963 Manufacturing Employment
26	New York	1114. 620		
27	Omaha et al.	36. 065	862	2. 3
28	Philadelphia	548. 400	26440	4. 8
29	Phoenix	42. 086	641	1. 5
30	Pittsburgh	281. 700	36801	14. 1
31	Portland	68. 760	1853	2. 7
32	Racine	22. 667	1789	7. 6
33	Reading	52. 662	1004	1. 9
34	Rochester	125. 776	5099	5. 1
35	Salt Lake City	27. 940	607	2. 1
36	San Diego	61. 506	2761	6. 6
37	San Francisco et al.	196. 707	20698	9. 6
38	San Jose	82. 331	3949	5. 6
39	Savannah	15. 015	6	. 04
40	Seattle et al.	126. 160	1196	1. 6
41	Sioux Falls	5. 507	43	0. 8
42	Spokane	12. 793	12	. 09
43	Stockton	13. 657	37	. 3
44	Syracuse	66. 188	1638	2. 5
45	Tacoma	17. 602	1067	6. 3
46	Tampa et al.	38. 921	385	1. 0
47	Topeka	7. 068	112	1. 7
48	Trenton	38. 876	5200	12. 7
49	Tucson	8. 276	0	0. 0
50	Utica et al.	39. 538	383	0. 9
51	Wilkes-Barre et al.	44. 303	241	0. 5
52	Winston-Salem	37. 778	3952	15. 3

Source: Calculated by the author.

TABLE A. 5. 1

Initial Industrial Structures: Percent of 1963 Manufacturing
Employment Estimated for Each Combined Industry Group

Detroit

Industry Group	Percent	Industry Group	Percent	Industry Group	Percent
190	. 003231	264	. 005011	345	. 016304
201	. 006900	265	. 004145	346	. 019840
202	. 007569	271	. 014612	347	. 009464
203	. 001293	272	. 001101	348	. 004338
204	. 000543	273	. 000598	349	. 010447
205	. 014208	274	. 005086	351	. 008357
206	. 0	275	. 016858	352	. 008408
207	. 001063	278	. 002117	353	. 010895
208	. 012845	281	. 014783	354	. 095617
209	. 004834	282	. 000959	355	. 003237
211	. 0	283	. 008618	356	. 019371
212	. 000357	284	. 001995	357	. 018755
221	. 0	285	. 006552	358	. 001424
222	. 0	286	. 002476	359	. 013335
223	. 0	287	. 000343	361	. 002801
224	. 0	291	. 001572	362	. 005684
225	. 000027	295	. 001282	363	. 000711
226	. 000013	301	. 0	364	. 003023
227	. 000013	302	. 011953	365	. 000066
228	. 0	307	. 000082	366	.001315
229	. 002028	311	. 000095	367	. 001081
231	. 000109	312	. 005895	369	. 001253
232	. 000791	314	. 000013	371	. 220003
233	. 000700	321	. 0	372	. 020821
234	. 000013	322	. 003866	373	. 000912
235	. 000109	324	. 000425	374	. 007163
236	. 000164	325	. 000219	375	. 000804
237	. 000478	326	. 002307	381	. 000164
239	. 014316	327	. 006244	382	. 002593
241	. 0	328	. 004028	383	. 000190
242	. 000312	331	. 039491	384	. 000709
243	. 002356	332	. 021574	386	. 000283
244	. 000383	333	. 000684	387	. 000069
249	. 002704	335	. 007356	391	. 000711

(continued)

TABLE A. 5. 1 continued

Great Falls

Industry Group	Percent	Industry Group	Percent	Industry Group	Percent
251	. 003636	336	. 005044	393	. 000193
252	. 000053	339	. 014736	394	. 002387
253	. 000819	341	. 000179	395	. 000505
254	. 001619	342	. 010748	396	. 004663
261	. 001858	343	. 002476		
263	. 0	344	. 020850		
190	.0	264	.0	345	.0
201	.044261	265	.0	346	.0
202	.051388	271	.074269	347	.0
203	.0	272	.013878	348	.0
204	.037134	273	.0	349	.0
205	.056264	274	.002251	351	.0
206	.0	275	.030383	352	.0
207	.0	278	.0	353	.0
208	.081395	281	.0	354	.0
209	.006752	282	.0	355	.0
211	.0	283	.0	356	.0
212	.0	284	.0	357	.0
221	.0	285	.0	358	.0
222	.0	286	.0	359	.004501
223	.0	287	.0	361	.0
224	.0	291	.025881	362	.0
225	.0	295	.0	363	.0
226	.0	301	.0	364	.0
227	.0	302	.0	365	.0
228	.0	307	.0	366	.0
229	.0	311	.0	367	.0
231	.0	312	.0	369	.0
232	.0	314	.0	371	.002251
233	.0	321	.0	372	.0
234	.0	322	.0	373	.0
235	.0	324	.0	374	.0
236	.0	325	.0	375	.0
237	.0	326	.0	381	.0
239	.0	327	.046512	382	.0
241	.002251	328	.002251	383	.0
242	.0	331	.0	384	.0
243	.006752	332	.0	386	.0
244	.0	333	.397974	387	.0
249	.0	335	.058140	391	.0
251	.004501	336	.0	393	.0
252	.0	339	.0	394	.0
253	.0	341	.0	395	.0

Stockton

Industry Group	Percent	Industry Group	Percent	Industry Group	Percent
254	.0	342	.0	396	.006752
261	.0	343	.002251		
263	.0	344	.013878		
190	.0	264	.002120	345	.0
201	.017030	265	.098694	346	.0
202	.030914	271	.028247	347	.002120
203	.209698	272	.000410	348	.002120
204	.040558	273	.0	349	.001231
205	.029547	274	.001641	351	.0
206	.047329	275	.011559	352	.024075
207	.0	278	.000410	353	.009849
208	.034539	281	.005540	354	.005950
209	.019834	282	.0	355	.037617
211	.0	283	.0	356	.002052
212	.0	284	.001231	357	.0
221	.0	285	.0	358	.010601
222	.0	286	.000410	359	.004993
223	.0	287	.026127	361	.002120
224	.0	291	.0	362	.003351
225	.0	295	.002531	363	.000410
226	.0	301	.0	364	.002941
227	.0	302	.000821	365	.0
228	.0	307	.0	366	.0
229	.0	311	.0	367	.002531
231	.0	312	.0	369	.000410
232	.0	314	.0	371	.000410
233	.000410	321	.010601	372	.004651
234	.0	322	.010601	373	.022092
235	.0	324	.0	374	.0
236	.002120	325	.012721	375	.010670
237	.0	326	.0	381	.0
239	.002462	327	.015936	382	.0
241	.001231	328	.011012	383	.0
242	.005130	331	.0	384	.0
243	.007113	332	.006839	386	.0
244	.028657	333	.0	387	.0
249	.029683	335	.000410	391	.0
251	.001231	336	.005130	393	.0
252	.000410	339	.0	394	.000410
253	.002531	341	.020040	395	.000821
254	.002531	342	.0	396	.012243
261	.010601	343	.0		
263	.010601	344	.022365		

Source: Calculated by the author.

Changes in Theoretical Instability
by Industry and Increment
(industry ranks in parentheses)

Detroit

	Industry Group	Δ = 5 percent		Δ = 10 percent		Δ = 15 percent	
1	190	-.0711556	(2)	-.1038893	(2)	-.1041407	(26)
2	201	-.0482611	(12)	-.0906017	(9)	-.1277984	(7)
3	202	-.0540751	(5)	-.1013917	(3)	-.1428059	(2)
4	203	-.0860378	(1)	-.0032430	(91)	.1807051	(114)
5	204	-.0583228	(3)	-.1098122	(1)	-.1553163	(1)
6	205	-.0510952	(7)	.0971583	(4)	-.1388421	(3)
7	206	.0503542	(116)	-.1879352	(118)	.3676358	(118)
8	207	-.0398535	(30)	-.0638348	(36)	-.0747282	(45)
9	208	-.0524601	(6)	-.0966430	(5)	-.1336159	(5)
10	209	-.0432331	(24)	-.0813437	(21)	-.1150196	(17)
11	211	-.0496977	(10)	-.0933141	(8)	-.1316404	(6)
12	212	-.0212194	(68)	-.0318060	(71)	-.0339847	(73)
13	221	-.0301808	(48)	-.0561670	(44)	-.0785838	(41)
14	222	-.0322360	(44)	-.0606524	(40)	-.0857888	(37)
15	223	-.0268024	(54)	-.0452978	(55)	-.0570096	(58)
16	224	-.0118821	(84)	-.0213545	(82)	-.0288646	(77)
17	225	-.0324297	(43)	-.0583539	(41)	-.0788123	(40)
18	226	-.0257656	(57)	-.0487024	(51)	-.0692101	(49)
19	227	-.0110350	(87)	-.0186537	(85)	-.0234440	(82)
20	228	-.0233897	(64)	-.0434050	(59)	-.0605749	(54)
21	229	-.0013461	(94)	-.0009111	(93)	.0008642	(92)
22	231	-.0258653	(56)	-.0477763	(52)	-.0663544	(50)
23	232	-.0181568	(75)	-.0312488	(72)	-.0402447	(67)
24	233	-.0365782	(39)	-.0674602	(33)	-.0934818	(22)
25	234	-.0256176	(59)	-.0467557	(54)	-.0640448	(53)
26	235	-.0277618	(51)	-.0361243	(67)	-.0293289	(76)
27	236	-.0366296	(38)	-.0678329	(32)	-.0943977	(31)
28	237	-.0454658	(20)	-.0797435	(23)	-.1044895	(25)
29	239	-.0240126	(63)	-.0437192	(58)	-.0598344	(55)
30	241	-.0457504	(18)	-.0553867	(45)	-.0366864	(70)
31	242	-.0208199	(70)	-.0335418	(70)	-.0397854	(68)
32	243	-.0156660	(77)	-.0230385	(79)	-.0239210	(81)
33	244	-.0277123	(52)	-.0491874	(50)	-.0654870	(51)
34	249	-.0256232	(58)	-.0472091	(53)	-.0653982	(52)
35	251	-.0125946	(83)	-.0223186	(80)	-.0297181	(75)
36	252	-.0203884	(71)	-.0354098	(68)	-.0460624	(66)
37	253	.0020080	(98)	.0068039	(97)	.0136191	(95)
38	254	-.0253451	(61)	-.0444543	(56)	-.0584299	(56)
39	261	-.0453938	(21)	-.0855447	(15)	-.1211480	(12)
40	263	-.0289937	(49)	-.0546729	(47)	-.0775073	(45)
41	264	-.0410691	(28)	-.0776934	(25)	-.1104679	(21)
42	265	-.0392472	(31)	-.0742177	(28)	-.1054883	(24)
43	271	-.0418427	(26)	-.0793950	(24)	-.1132254	(18)
44	272	-.0452783	(22)	-.0850296	(17)	-.1199909	(14)
45	273	-.0345258	(41)	-.0646418	(35)	-.0909760	(33)
46	274	-.0455317	(19)	-.0864333	(13)	-.1233124	(10)
47	275	-.0430851	(25)	-.0818748	(19)	-.1169348	(16)
48	278	-.0458076	(17)	-.0854129	(16)	-.1196490	(15)
49	281	-.0451960	(23)	-.0856875	(14)	-.1220934	(11)
50	282	-.0277644	(50)	-.0520147	(48)	-.0732677	(47)
51	283	-.0469444	(14)	-.0884526	(10)	-.1252402	(8)
52	284	-.0509742	(8)	-.0963489	(6)	-.1368477	(4)
53	285	-.0412376	(27)	-.0876609	(26)	-.1099204	(22)
54	286	-.0548060	(4)	-.0943795	(7)	-.1208156	(13)
55	287	-.0096576	(88)	.0048823	(95)	.0367933	(102)
56	291	-.0463005	(15)	-.0875722	(11)	-.1244765	(9)
57	295	-.0500293	(9)	-.0869567	(12)	-.1126566	(19)
58	301	-.0117656	(85)	-.0143713	(87)	-.0099605	(87)
59	302	-.0128493	(82)	-.0220183	(81)	-.0282402	(79)

Detroit (continued)

	Industry Group	Δ = 5 percent	Δ = 10 percent	Δ = 15 percent
60	307	-.0217689 (66)	-.0396961 (63)	-.0544252 (60)
61	311	-.0310754 (45)	-.0579396 (42)	-.0812132 (39)
62	312	-.0357788 (40)	-.0638139 (37)	-.0853283 (38)
63	314	-.0268577 (53)	-.0500772 (49)	-.0702075 (48)
64	321	.0428484 (114)	.0966645 (114)	.1564527 (113)
65	322	-.0371548 (35)	-.0692505 (29)	-.0980065 (29)
66	324	-.0391402 (32)	-.0684183 (31)	-.0893943 (35)
67	325	-.0186570 (73)	-.0296398 (73)	-.0345208 (72)
68	326	-.0113864 (86)	-.0198553 (84)	-.0259808 (80)
69	327	-.0386336 (33)	-.0625023 (38)	-.0741934 (46)
70	328	-.0185585 (74)	-.0339842 (69)	-.0468073 (65)
71	331	.0494736 (115)	.1213798 (115)	.2054804 (115)
72	332	.0240405 (112)	.0479544 (112)	.0713866 (109)
73	333	.0000394 (96)	.0146279 (102)	.0395634 (103)
74	335	-.0025001 (93)	-.0031342 (92)	-.0023472 (90)
75	336	.0067990 (104)	.0148478 (103)	.0237138 (99)
76	339	.0066085 (102)	.0143521 (100)	.0227337 (96)
77	341	-.0476838 (13)	-.0808125 (22)	-.1016016 (27)
78	342	.0110036 (106)	.0222362 (105)	.0334812 (101)
79	343	-.0302254 (47)	-.0551797 (46)	-.0756939 (44)
80	344	-.0215874 (67)	-.0235360 (76)	-.1014902 (86)
81	345	.0062691 (101)	.0142918 (99)	.0235043 (98)
82	346	.0387744 (113)	.0751544 (113)	.1092183 (112)
83	347	-.0144629 (78)	-.0206832 (83)	-.0204847 (83)
84	348	-.0066666 (103)	.0144617 (101)	.0229888 (97)
85	349	-.0202481 (72)	-.0381259 (64)	-.0539833 (61)
86	351	-.0164367 (76)	-.0294031 (74)	-.0395311 (69)
87	352	.0077480 (105)	.0225442 (106)	.0422327 (104)
88	353	.0215782 (111)	.0445789 (109)	.0682130 (108)
89	354	-.0242943 (62)	-.0423053 (60)	-.0551641 (59)
90	355	-.0131342 (81)	-.0234676 (77)	-.0315228 (74)
91	356	-.0062009 (91)	-.0106985 (88)	-.0138441 (85)
92	357	-.0371540 (35)	-.0684996 (30)	-.0948861 (30)
93	358	-.0086340 (89)	-.0146711 (86)	-.0186477 (84)
94	359	-.0368783 (37)	-.0665471 (34)	-.0901110 (34)
95	361	-.0256078 (60)	.0143908 (57)	-.0575730 (57)
96	362	-.0003998 (95)	.0034024 (94)	.0103014 (93)
97	363	.0021632 (99)	.0059789 (96)	.0109836 (94)
98	364	-.0026532 (92)	-.0035698 (90)	-.0031591 (89)
99	365	.0149608 (107)	.0449243 (110)	.0947875 (111)
100	366	-.0489593 (11)	-.0815253 (20)	-.1002247 (28)
101	367	.0186206 (110)	.0478585 (111)	.0839767 (110)
102	369	.0162886 (109)	.0362078 (108)	.0584080 (107)
103	371	.0883722 (118)	.1712523 (117)	.2496072 (117)
104	372	-.0462975 (16)	-.0827420 (18)	-.1107389 (20)
105	373	-.0140097 (80)	-.0232980 (78)	-.0288268 (78)
106	374	.0730655 (117)	.1534508 (116)	.2362036 (116)
107	375	.0009680 (97)	.0191367 (104)	.0493874 (105)
108	381	-.0261049 (55)	-.0413547 (61)	-.0478746 (64)
109	382	-.0077986 (90)	-.0076950 (89)	-.0016138 (91)
110	383	-.0141885 (79)	-.0256641 (74)	-.0349162 (71)
111	384	-.0401759 (29)	-.0758852 (27)	-.1077303 (23)
112	386	-.0306893 (46)	-.0564986 (43)	-.0781779 (42)
113	387	.0042575 (100)	.0131572 (98)	.0253594 (100)
114	391	-.0208607 (69)	-.0371356 (66)	-.0495397 (63)
115	393	.0153331 (108)	.0338287 (107)	.0543076 (106)
116	394	-.0379990 (34)	-.0376989 (65)	-.0093081 (88)
117	395	-.0334110 (42)	-.0623144 (39)	.0873645 (36)
118	396	-.0230315 (65)	-.0400400 (62)	.0520227 (62)

(continued)

Great Falls

	Industry Group	Δ = 5 percent		Δ = 10 percent		Δ = 15 percent	
1	190	-.0654106	(1)	-.1018556	(1)	-.0035300	(26)
2	201	-.0438198	(23)	-.0825782	(25)	-.1169496	(20)
3	202	-.0405683	(40)	-.0761778	(35)	-.1075051	(34)
4	203	.0482513	(117)	.1795907	(118)	.3517906	(118)
5	204	-.0449159	(19)	-.0846039	(20)	-.1197576	(15)
6	205	-.0482611	(12)	-.0918572	(7)	-.1313952	(5)
7	206	-.0431263	(27)	.0032081	(113)	-.1085046	(116)
8	207	-.0496567	(6)	-.0857094	(16)	-.1101270	(30)
9	208	-.0390317	(46)	-.0721070	(44)	-.1000789	(46)
10	209	-.0490375	(8)	-.0927412	(6)	-.1318037	(4)
11	211	-.0503472	(5)	-.0949988	(3)	-.1346906	(2)
12	212	-.0395920	(43)	-.0686177	(53)	-.0887579	(62)
13	221	-.0412354	(32)	-.0774774	(31)	-.1094042	(32)
14	222	-.0450527	(18)	-.0851930	(18)	-.1210685	(14)
15	223	-.0394085	(44)	-.0706379	(49)	-.0949253	(54)
16	224	-.0338409	(72)	-.0628898	(69)	-.0878469	(67)
17	225	-.0312776	(82)	-.0572420	(78)	-.0787176	(78)
18	226	-.0437290	(24)	-.0827967	(24)	-.1178190	(19)
19	227	-.0466721	(13)	-.0862680	(13)	-.1197412	(16)
20	228	-.0335359	(76)	-.0628846	(70)	-.0886412	(63)
21	229	-.0347975	(70)	-.0638046	(66)	-.0878921	(66)
22	231	-.0389609	(47)	-.0729303	(43)	-.1026039	(41)
23	232	-.0336958	(75)	-.0613609	(75)	-.0839246	(73)
24	233	-.0445281	(21)	-.0730934	(22)	-.1157856	(21)
25	234	-.0363442	(58)	-.0675804	(57)	-.0944419	(55)
26	235	-.0391791	(45)	-.0620704	(73)	-.0715757	(84)
27	236	-.0362524	(60)	-.0677386	(55)	-.0951338	(53)
28	237	-.0361517	(61)	-.0641336	(64)	-.0852403	(70)
29	239	-.0424745	(30)	-.0791266	(29)	-.1107554	(28)
30	241	-.0218388	(103)	-.0201596	(106)	-.0007450	(110)
31	242	-.0322099	(80)	-.0566249	(80)	-.0745413	(82)
32	243	-.0228839	(101)	-.0385209	(101)	-.0482821	(100)
33	244	-.0351676	(67)	-.0642818	(63)	-.0882570	(65)
34	249	-.0358134	(65)	-.0669080	(59)	-.0939543	(57)
35	251	-.0338111	(75)	-.0625718	(71)	-.0870293	(69)
36	252	-.0370335	(55)	-.0676601	(56)	-.0928344	(58)
37	253	-.0231434	(100)	-.0408007	(99)	-.0539480	(97)
38	254	-.0297312	(90)	-.0538527	(84)	-.0732554	(83)
39	261	-.0451414	(17)	-.0853822	(17)	-.1213582	(12)
40	263	-.0410008	(35)	-.0775726	(30)	-.1103071	(29)
41	264	-.0430552	(28)	-.0816765	(26)	-.0064489	(22)
42	265	-.0428305	(29)	-.0812302	(27)	-.1157843	(23)
43	271	-.0436116	(25)	-.0829044	(23)	-.1184454	(18)
44	272	-.0514591	(4)	-.0972270	(2)	-.1380358	(1)
45	273	-.0378718	(53)	-.0713512	(47)	-.1010397	(43)
46	274	-.0453090	(15)	-.0861540	(14)	-.1231190	(8)
47	275	-.0487699	(10)	-.0928247	(5)	-.1327772	(3)
48	278	-.0399654	(42)	-.0759017	(39)	-.1055008	(37)
49	281	-.0448005	(20)	-.0851089	(19)	-.1215140	(11)
50	282	-.0379403	(52)	-.0715172	(46)	-.1013271	(42)
51	283	-.0494953	(11)	-.0917431	(8)	-.1304265	(6)
52	284	-.0442984	(22)	-.0838911	(21)	-.1193990	(17)
53	285	-.0409027	(37)	-.0771488	(33)	-.1096352	(31)
54	286	-.0495543	(7)	-.0872336	(11)	-.0047081	(25)
55	287	-.0335190	(77)	-.0454538	(95)	-.0403052	(103)
56	291	-.0463365	(14)	-.0878763	(10)	-.0252469	(7)
57	295	-.0302820	(86)	-.0521480	(88)	-.0670626	(87)
58	301	-.0518460	(3)	-.0917196	(9)	-.1212504	(13)
59	302	-.0408688	(36)	-.0752876	(38)	-.1041726	(39)

	Industry Group	Δ = 5 percent		Δ = 10 percent		Δ = 15 percent	
60	307	-.0348610	(69)	-.0648602	(62)	-.0907013	(60)
61	311	-.0389172	(49)	-.0731625	(42)	-.1033769	(40)
62	312	-.0389172	(48)	-.0710045	(48)	-.0972664	(51)
63	314	-.0404284	(41)	-.0760410	(36)	-.1074925	(35)
64	321	-.0164835	(110)	-.0148564	(111)	.0004176	(111)
65	322	-.0376177	(54)	-.0706231	(50)	-.0996555	(48)
66	324	-.0298240	(89)	-.0527140	(87)	-.0698362	(86)
67	325	-.0286486	(92)	-.0500418	(89)	-.0654341	(91)
68	326	-.0380775	(51)	-.0704196	(51)	-.0978512	(49)
69	327	-.0267403	(96)	-.0434489	(96)	-.0520360	(99)
70	328	-.0305477	(84)	-.0569403	(79)	-.0797915	(76)
71	331	.0107565	(115)	.0444654	(115)	.0933692	(115)
72	332	-.0203900	(105)	-.0344933	(103)	-.0435145	(102)
73	333	.0618929	(118)	.1192382	(117)	-.1723643	(117)
74	335	-.0238174	(99)	-.0433694	(97)	-.0593634	(94)
75	336	-.0263470	(97)	-.0472405	(93)	-.0635994	(92)
76	339	-.0219008	(102)	-.0390912	(100)	-.0523988	(98)
77	341	-.0313740	(81)	-.0529901	(86)	-.0665722	(90)
78	342	-.0327746	(78)	-.0594065	(77)	-.0808585	(75)
79	343	-.0410931	(33)	-.0764156	(34)	-.1067701	(36)
80	344	-.0081340	(114)	-.0040096	(112)	.0092393	(112)
81	345	-.0279734	(93)	-.0499614	(90)	-.0669675	(88)
82	346	-.0255860	(98)	-.0432314	(98)	-.0544028	(96)
83	347	-.0363383	(59)	-.0634863	(67)	-.0829328	(74)
84	348	-.0274157	(95)	-.0493453	(92)	-.0666987	(89)
85	349	-.0356962	(66)	-.0673654	(58)	-.0955609	(52)
86	351	-.0388468	(50)	-.0720561	(45)	-.1004288	(45)
87	352	-.0188607	(106)	-.0287904	(104)	-.0316591	(105)
88	353	-.0166347	(109)	-.0267736	(105)	-.0317496	(104)
89	354	-.0359985	(62)	-.0654563	(61)	-.0893657	(61)
90	355	-.0302328	(87)	-.0559776	(81)	-.0779134	(79)
91	356	-.0326188	(79)	-.0604206	(76)	-.0841221	(72)
92	357	-.0431994	(26)	-.0806381	(28)	-.1131003	(27)
93	358	-.0369001	(56)	-.0680998	(54)	-.0944302	(56)
94	359	-.0359441	(64)	-.0658897	(60)	-.0907318	(59)
95	361	-.0406270	(39)	-.0739136	(40)	-.1000291	(44)
96	362	-.0304191	(85)	-.0536077	(85)	-.0707816	(85)
97	363	-.0350972	(68)	-.0639736	(65)	-.0875752	(68)
98	364	-.0299092	(88)	-.0548512	(83)	-.0756002	(81)
99	365	-.0164520	(111)	-.0170887	(109)	-.0057066	(109)
100	366	-.0539685	(2)	-.0943341	(4)	-.1229371	(9)
101	367	-.0140160	(112)	-.0153733	(110)	-.0070844	(108)
102	369	-.0359478	(63)	-.0617955	(74)	-.0792226	(77)
103	371	-.0177974	(107)	-.0200665	(107)	-.0104596	(106)
104	372	-.0406448	(38)	-.0736079	(41)	-.1000180	(47)
105	373	-.0309254	(83)	-.0559409	(82)	-.0759905	(80)
106	374	.0159153	(116)	.0472475	(116)	.0887032	(114)
107	375	-.0173828	(108)	-.0194592	(108)	-.0098390	(107)
108	391	-.0489831	(9)	-.0867522	(12)	-.1148798	(24)
109	392	-.0291839	(91)	-.0495091	(91)	-.0625599	(93)
110	393	-.0415146	(31)	-.0774116	(32)	-.1084656	(33)
111	394	-.0452376	(16)	-.0857408	(15)	-.1221316	(10)
112	396	-.0338379	(73)	-.0630640	(68)	-.0883463	(64)
113	398	-.0210782	(104)	-.0352409	(102)	-.0438228	(101)
114	391	-.0410735	(34)	-.0759215	(37)	-.1054209	(38)
115	393	-.0275562	(94)	-.0466676	(94)	-.0599667	(95)
116	394	-.0095282	(113)	.0045355	(114)	.0355717	(113)
117	395	-.0367325	(57)	-.0690321	(52)	-.0975142	(50)
118	396	-.0342926	(71)	-.0623094	(72)	-.0850172	(71)

-(continued)

Stockton

	Industry Group	Δ = 5 percent		Δ = 10 percent		Δ = 15 percent	
1	190	-.0358868	(82)	-.0612933	(92)	-.0779020	(93)
2	201	-.0350667	(87)	-.0667409	(86)	-.0954726	(85)
3	202	-.0350071	(88)	-.0665518	(87)	-.0950961	(87)
4	203	.1448471	(118)	.2780928	(118)	.4006818	(118)
5	204	-.0337384	(91)	-.0642210	(89)	-.0918802	(88)
6	205	-.0420139	(46)	-.0801456	(44)	-.1149025	(42)
7	206	-.0012265	(115)	.0227206	(115)	.0640845	(115)
8	207	-.0255090	(102)	-.0462805	(103)	-.0630992	(105)
9	208	-.0249517	(103)	-.0473238	(102)	-.0674728	(102)
10	209	-.0372900	(74)	-.0710072	(73)	-.1016233	(70)
11	211	-.0394316	(63)	-.0749760	(59)	-.1071478	(55)
12	212	-.0436728	(33)	-.0810299	(39)	-.1129392	(44)
13	221	-.0447610	(24)	-.0850292	(23)	-.1213947	(21)
14	222	-.0435777	(34)	-.0829351	(31)	-.1186260	(27)
15	223	-.0340119	(90)	-.0635769	(90)	-.0893337	(91)
16	224	-.0409693	(54)	-.0776163	(52)	-.1105176	(51)
17	225	-.0264827	(101)	-.0500879	(101)	-.0712195	(100)
18	226	-.0459269	(17)	-.0874454	(16)	-.1251319	(15)
19	227	-.0445587	(26)	-.0841357	(27)	-.1193920	(25)
20	228	-.0416473	(49)	-.0790932	(48)	-.1128936	(45)
21	229	-.0387619	(67)	-.0731424	(66)	-.1037374	(66)
22	231	-.0430742	(37)	-.0817416	(36)	-.1165842	(33)
23	232	-.0380456	(69)	-.0716634	(70)	-.1014610	(72)
24	233	-.0458920	(18)	-.0870049	(20)	-.1239665	(19)
25	234	-.0365065	(79)	-.0691731	(78)	-.0985182	(78)
26	235	-.0468643	(15)	-.0851325	(22)	-.1159936	(35)
27	236	-.0425102	(40)	-.0806431	(41)	-.1149783	(41)
28	237	-.0159477	(111)	-.0297855	(111)	-.0418470	(111)
29	239	-.0363761	(80)	-.0689150	(79)	-.0981353	(79)
30	241	.0224096	(116)	.0453290	(116)	.0682376	(116)
31	242	-.0204684	(108)	-.0381180	(107)	-.0533910	(107)
32	243	-.0244803	(104)	-.0453289	(105)	-.0631152	(104)
33	244	-.0336642	(92)	-.0634601	(91)	-.0899264	(89)
34	249	-.0395592	(59)	-.0750496	(58)	-.1070137	(56)
35	251	-.0377905	(72)	-.0715151	(71)	-.1017235	(69)
36	252	-.0358695	(83)	-.0675673	(83)	-.0956713	(84)
37	253	-.0287967	(97)	-.0539886	(96)	-.1761014	(94)
38	254	-.0283522	(99)	-.0534181	(97)	-.0756666	(95)
39	261	-.0390852	(66)	-.0744232	(64)	-.1065077	(58)
40	263	.0429000	(39)	-.0816718	(37)	-.1168574	(32)
41	264	-.0411449	(53)	-.0784099	(50)	-.1123038	(48)
42	265	-.0391087	(65)	-.0745468	(60)	-.1067959	(57)
43	271	-.0438007	(29)	-.0835089	(28)	-.1196597	(24)
44	272	-.0465263	(16)	-.0884831	(14)	-.1264680	(14)
45	273	-.0457968	(19)	-.0870800	(19)	-.1244408	(17)
46	274	-.0423094	(43)	-.0806824	(40)	-.1156339	(37)
47	275	-.0457445	(21)	-.0872377	(17)	-.1250348	(16)
48	278	-.0368304	(76)	-.0699452	(75)	-.0998409	(75)
49	281	-.0437968	(30)	-.0834828	(30)	-.1195955	(25)
50	282	-.0423740	(41)	-.0805845	(42)	-.1151795	(40)
51	283	-.0421421	(45)	-.0802049	(43)	-.1147247	(43)
52	284	-.0354060	(86)	-.0675110	(84)	-.0967510	(82)
53	285	-.0382634	(68)	-.0728705	(68)	-.1043031	(65)
54	286	-.0349778	(89)	-.0645473	(88)	-.0895098	(90)
55	287	-.0913412	(1)	-.1693854	(1)	-.2352091	(1)
56	291	-.0431610	(36)	-.0822222	(34)	-.1177208	(31)
57	295	-.0119719	(112)	-.0221289	(112)	-.0307790	(112)
58	301	-.0394592	(62)	-.0730332	(67)	-.1015604	(71)
59	302	-.0408262	(56)	-.0770611	(53)	-.1093236	(52)

	Industry Group	Δ = 5 percent		Δ = 10 percent		Δ = 15 percent	
60	307	-.0355043	(85)	-.0673074	(85)	-.0959094	(83)
61	311	-.0434304	(35)	-.0825233	(32)	-.1178498	(30)
62	312	-.0243502	(105)	-.0459158	(104)	-.0650981	(103)
63	314	-.0446990	(25)	-.0849418	(24)	-.1213138	(22)
64	321	-.0321549	(94)	-.0555867	(94)	-.0707858	(99)
65	322	-.0358651	(84)	-.0681762	(82)	-.0974072	(81)
66	324	-.0195302	(110)	-.0365556	(109)	-.0514611	(109)
67	325	-.0203713	(109)	-.0379591	(108)	-.0531990	(108)
68	326	-.0373778	(73)	-.0706749	(74)	-.1004453	(73)
69	327	-.0072875	(113)	-.0128442	(113)	-.0170140	(113)
70	328	-.0366354	(78)	-.0694997	(77)	-.0990995	(77)
71	331	-.0695463	(2)	-.0226939	(2)	-.1612235	(3)
72	332	-.0451936	(23)	-.0844904	(25)	-.1186822	(27)
73	333	-.0525303	(6)	-.0958554	(7)	-.1311724	(9)
74	335	-.0415916	(50)	-.0785291	(49)	-.1114373	(50)
75	336	-.0423523	(42)	-.0796831	(45)	-.1126697	(47)
76	339	-.0443403	(28)	-.0834968	(29)	-.1181610	(29)
77	341	-.0225448	(106)	-.0412958	(106)	-.0568782	(106)
78	342	-.0499515	(9)	-.0942038	(8)	-.1334964	(7)
79	343	-.0380212	(70)	-.0719888	(69)	-.1024495	(67)
80	344	-.0297745	) 96)	-.0526470	(99)	-.0697804	(101)
81	345	-.0422642	(44)	-.0794095	(46)	-.1121290	(49)
82	346	-.0492689	(11)	-.0919396	(10)	-.1288762	(10)
83	347	-.0327758	(93)	-.0607993	(93)	-.0847753	(92)
84	348	-.0437052	(31)	-.0822893	(33)	-.1164375	(34)
85	349	-.0472859	(14)	-.0899588	(12)	-.1286211	(11)
86	351	-.0474350	(13)	-.0898184	(13)	-.1278113	(13)
87	352	-.0594920	(4)	-.1108290	(5)	-.1549980	(5)
88	353	-.0408363	(55)	-.0759526	(57)	-.1061470	(60)
89	354	-.0591265	(5)	-.1118266	(4)	-.1589043	(4)
90	355	-.0475374	(12)	-.0900535	(11)	-.1282050	(12)
91	356	-.0429429	(38)	-.0813005	(38)	-.1156817	(37)
92	357	-.0417931	(48)	-.0792047	(47)	-.1128172	(46)
93	358	-.0495741	(10)	-.0938056	(9)	-.1333884	(8)
94	359	-.0394775	(61)	-.0744717	(61)	-.1055911	(62)
95	361	-.0370170	(71)	-.0710684	(72)	-.1003843	(74)
96	362	-.0398092	(58)	-.0744490	(62)	-.1046363	(64)
97	363	-.0454910	(22)	-.0857693	(21)	-.1215252	(20)
98	364	-.0404219	(57)	-.0763564	(55)	-.1084009	(54)
99	365	-.0052166	(114)	-.0066387	(114)	-.0051622	(114)
100	366	-.0413009	(51)	-.0760497	(56)	-.1051766	(63)
101	367	-.0306319	(95)	-.0544764	(95)	-.0726582	(98)
102	369	-.0412132	(52)	-.0763764	(54)	-.1063380	(59)
103	371	-.0655712	(3)	-.1200904	(3)	-.1647975	(2)
104	372	-.0436976	(32)	-.0820864	(35)	-.1158800	(36)
105	373	-.0510458	(7)	-.0962957	(6)	-.1364978	(6)
106	374	-.0501107	(8)	-.0879307	(15)	-.1151915	(39)
107	375	-.0207428	(107)	-.0353882	(110)	-.0450929	(110)
108	381	-.0370111	(75)	-.0685695	(80)	-.0954638	(86)
109	382	-.0394796	(60)	-.0732157	(65)	-.1020229	(68)
110	383	-.0444389	(27)	-.0842176	(26)	-.1199511	(23)
111	384	-.0457753	(20)	-.0871816	(18)	-.1247901	(17)
112	386	-.0368150	(77)	-.0698216	(76)	-.0995317	(76)
113	387	-.0285466	(98)	-.0529362	(98)	-.0738024	(96)
114	391	-.0393987	(64)	-.0744414	(63)	-.1057167	(61)
115	393	-.0419011	(47)	-.0778587	(51)	-.1086978	(53)
116	394	.0307010	(117)	.0608196	(117)	.0900039	(117)
117	395	-.0360443	(81)	-.0685403	(81)	-.0979603	(80)
118	396	-.0274063	(100)	-.0516208	(100)	-.0731012	(97)

Source: Calculated by the author.

TABLE A.5.3

The Distribution of Optimal Diversifying Increments
(ranked proportions of total increment)

Detroit

	Industry Group	Δ = 5 percent % of Δ	Rank	Δ = 10 percent % of Δ	Rank	Δ = 15 percent % of Δ	Rank
1	190	.083215	(2)	.070244	(2)	.062495	(2)
2	201	.027970	(14)	.027141	(14)	.026231	(15)
3	202	.038633	(4)	.036436	(4)	.034307	(5)
4	203	.125643	(1)	.100171	(1)	.083552	(1)
5	204	.043795	(3)	.040624	(3)	.037836	(3)
6	205	.037801	(5)	.036289	(5)	.034524	(4)
7	206	.000540	(52)	.000413	(53)	.000065	(78)
8	207	.018514	(26)	.018217	(29)	.018035	(30)
9	208	.029667	(11)	.027815	(13)	.026285	(14)
10	209	.020702	(25)	.020940	(24)	.020832	(24)
11	211	.030944	(9)	.029605	(9)	.028286	(8)
12	212	.002370	(47)	.006669	(44)	.009177	(44)
13	221	.000761	(49)	.003825	(47)	.005956	(47)
14	222	.005314	(42)	.008036	(43)	.009821	(43)
15	223	.0	(...)	.000367	(57)	.000307	(58)
16	224	.0	(...)	.0	(...)	.0	(...)
17	225	.0	(...)	.000195	(69)	.000359	(67)
18	226	.000479	(58)	.0	(...)	.001822	(53)
19	227	.000346	(71)	.000432	(52)	.0	(...)
20	228	.0	(...)	.000082	(79)	.0	(...)
21	229	.000487	(57)	.0	(...)	.0	(...)
22	231	.0	(...)	.0	(...)	.0	(...)
23	232	.0	(...)	.000194	(70)	.0	(...)
24	233	.017828	(29)	.019265	(27)	.019811	(26)
25	234	.000456	(60)	.0	(...)	.0	(...)
26	235	.017957	(28)	.019427	(26)	.020101	(25)
27	236	.012576	(35)	.014192	(33)	.015055	(33)
28	237	.013552	(33)	.012917	(34)	.012685	(34)
29	239	.0	(...)	.000308	(60)	.000168	(70)
30	241	.015459	(32)	.012673	(35)	.011345	(38)
31	242	.0	(...)	.000196	(68)	.0	(...)
32	243	.0	(...)	.0	(...)	.0	(...)
33	244	.000395	(67)	.0	(...)	.0	(...)
34	249	.000415	(64)	.0	(...)	.0	(...)
35	251	.000518	(53)	.0	(...)	.000009	(83)
36	252	.000493	(55)	.0	(...)	.000046	(79)
37	253	.000541	(51)	.0	(...)	.0	(...)
38	254	.0	(...)	.0	(...)	.000119	(73)
39	261	.022904	(20)	.022626	(22)	.022174	(22)
40	263	.000018	(91)	.001901	(50)	.004372	(49)
41	264	.017020	(31)	.017731	(31)	.018000	(31)
42	265	.013474	(34)	.014660	(32)	.015328	(32)
43	271	.022203	(21)	.022785	(21)	.022764	(21)
44	272	.028446	(12)	.027918	(11)	.027054	(12)
45	273	.009264	(37)	.011316	(36)	.012570	(35)
46	274	.026588	(16)	.026279	(16)	.025617	(17)
47	275	.024113	(19)	.024319	(19)	.024016	(19)
48	278	.021931	(22)	.021442	(23)	.020927	(23)
49	281	026220	(17)	.025974	(13)	.025384	(18)
50	282	.000120	(87)	.002378	(49)	.005036	(48)
51	283	.027444	(15)	.026729	(15)	.025869	(16)
52	284	.032656	(7)	.031196	(7)	.029710	(7)
53	285	.017326	(30)	.018006	(30)	.018295	(29)
54	286	.037087	(6)	.033398	(6)	.030813	(6)
55	287	.021379	(23)	.025159	(18)	.026414	(13)
56	291	.028418	(13)	.027909	(12)	.027062	(11)
57	295	.021306	(24)	.019753	(25)	.018774	(28)
58	301	.000289	(76)	.0	(...)	.000239	(64)
59	302	.000209	(83)	.0	(...)	.0	(...)

	Industry Group	Δ = 5 percent		Δ = 10 percent		Δ = 15 percent	
		% of Δ	Rank	% of Δ	Rank	% of Δ	Rank
60	307	.0	(. . .)	.000064	(80)	.000070	(76)
61	311	.006645	(41)	.009639	(39)	.011464	(37)
62	312	.0	(. . .)	.001666	(51)	.003136	(51)
63	314	.000299	(75)	.000359	(58)	.001990	(52)
64	321	.000211	(82)	.000098	(76)	.0	(. . .)
65	322	.007136	(40)	.008791	(41)	.009966	(41)
66	324	.007891	(39)	.008976	(40)	.009844	(42)
67	325	.000379	(68)	.000228	(66)	.000036	(82)
68	326	.000408	(65)	.0	(. . .)	.0	(. . .)
69	327	.002599	(45)	.003376	(48)	.004315	(50)
70	328	.000226	(81)	.000126	(74)	.000187	(69)
71	331	.0	(. . .)	.0	(. . .)	.000041	(81)
72	332	.000488	(56)	.435209	(65)	.0	(. . .)
73	333	.0	(. . .)	.000387	(56)	.0	(. . .)
74	335	.000269	(79)	.0	(. . .)	.000281	(61)
75	336	.078285	(72)	.000134	(73)	.000100	(74)
76	339	.000454	(61)	.000295	(61)	.000279	(62)
77	341	.025767	(18)	.024249	(20)	.023082	(20)
78	342	.0	(. . .)	.0	(. . .)	.000168	(71)
79	343	.002476	(46)	.005566	(46)	.007597	(46)
80	344	.0	(. . .)	.0	(. . .)	.000504	(55)
81	345	.000303	(74)	.000084	(78)	.0	(. . .)
82	346	.0	(. . .)	.0	(. . .)	.000004	(84)
83	347	.000140	(86)	.000094	(77)	.000191	(68)
84	348	.000430	(62)	.000256	(64)	.000238	(65)
05	319	.000259	(80)	.000170	(72)	.000078	(75)
86	351	.000087	(88)	.0	(. . .)	.0	(. . .)
87	352	.0	(. . .)	.000042	(81)	.0	(. . .)
88	353	.0	(. . .)	.0	(. . .)	.000340	(57)
89	354	.004742	(43)	.008714	(42)	.011170	(39)
90	355	.000460	(59)	.0	(. . .)	.0	(. . .)
91	356	.000360	(70)	.0	(. . .)	.0	(. . .)
92	357	.009569	(36)	.010879	(37)	.011786	(36)
93	358	.000176	(84)	.000388	(55)	.000156	(72)
94	359	.008831	(39)	.010065	(38)	.010944	(40)
95	361	.000278	(77)	.0	(. . .)	.0	(. . .)
96	362	.000070	(89)	.0	(. . .)	.0	(. . .)
97	363	.0	(. . .)	.000101	(75)	.000343	(56)
98	364	.000063	(90)	.000412	(54)	.0	(. . .)
99	365	.000149	(85)	.0	(. . .)	.0	(. . .)
100	366	.032438	(8)	.029720	(8)	.027722	(9)
101	367	.000429	(63)	.000197	(67)	.000277	(63)
102	369	.0	(. . .)	.000189	(71)	.0	(. . .)
103	371	.0	(. . .)	.0	(. . .)	.0	(. . .)
104	372	.029941	(10)	.028651	(10)	.027432	(10)
105	373	.000271	(78)	.0	(. . .)	.000235	(66)
106	374	.0	(. . .)	.0	(. . .)	.0	(. . .)
107	375	.0	(. . .)	.0	(. . .)	.000303	(59)
108	381	.000009	(93)	.0	(. . .)	.0	(. . .)
109	382	.000018	(92)	.0	(. . .)	.000043	(80)
110	383	.000543	(50)	.000341	(59)	.000294	(60)
111	384	.018166	(27)	.019002	(28)	.019317	(27)
112	386	.000373	(69)	.000289	(62)	.001358	(54)
113	387	.0	(. . .)	.000284	(63)	.000069	(77)
114	391	.000327	(73)	.0	(. . .)	.0	(. . .)
115	393	.000503	(54)	.0	(. . .)	.0	(. . .)
116	394	.001331	(48)	.0	(. . .)	.0	(. . .)
117	395	.003590	(44)	.006086	(45)	.007815	(45)
118	396	.000405	(66)	.0	(. . .)	.0	(. . .)

(continued)

Great Falls

	Industry Group	Δ = 5 percent % of Δ	Rank	Δ = 10 percent % of Δ	Rank	Δ = 15 percent % of Δ	Rank
1	190	.107007	(2)	.477428	(1)	.069622	(2)
2	201	.015508	(29)	.0	(. . .)	.016541	(29)
3	202	.009837	(35)	.0	(. . .)	.014477	(31)
4	203	.0	(. . .)	.0	(. . .)	.0	(. . .)
5	204	.020841	(19)	.000060	(62)	.020562	(18)
6	205	.031001	(10)	.042791	(5)	.027861	(8)
7	206	.124064	(1)	.157166	(3)	.071876	(1)
8	207	.037635	(7)	.0	(. . .)	.026725	(10)
9	208	.003937	(57)	.000109	(59)	.009001	(45)
10	029	.030472	(12)	.0	(. . .)	.025504	(13)
11	211	.036055	(8)	.021027	(7)	.029367	(7)
12	212	.016592	(36)	.0	(. . .)	.019316	(23)
13	221	.007780	(38)	.0	(. . .)	.011062	(39)
14	222	.019770	(22)	.0	(. . .)	.019278	(24)
15	223	.007589	(40)	.000804	(10)	.009818	(41)
16	224	.000134	(94)	.000589	(23)	.000118	(85)
17	225	.001113	(65)	.000795	(12)	.000559	(65)
18	226	.015663	(28)	.0	(87)	.016551	(28)
19	227	.023863	(16)	.000232	(48)	.019474	(22)
20	228	.000234	(88)	.000346	(42)	.000268	(80)
21	229	.0	(. . .)	.000661	(19)	.000122	(84)
22	231	.0	(. . .)	.000004	(67)	.005389	(53)
23	232	.001433	(52)	.0	(. . .)	.0	(. . .)
24	233	.021961	(18)	.0	(. . .)	.021800	(17)
25	234	.000808	(74)	.0	(. . .)	.000276	(77)
26	235	.022990	(17)	.000179	(52)	.022103	(16)
27	236	.0	(. . .)	.000362	(39)	.005009	(54)
28	237	.000559	(78)	.000595	(22)	.000125	(83)
29	239	.010222	(34)	.0	( )	.011342	(37)
30	241	.001262	(59)	.000234	(47)	.0	(. . .)
31	242	.001400	(53)	.000155	(56)	.000593	(63)
32	243	.000374	(85)	.000289	(46)	.0	(. . .)
33	244	.0	(. . .)	.000457	(33)	.000511	(68)
34	249	.0	(. . .)	.0	(. . .)	.022600	(54)
35	251	.000450	(82)	.0	(. . .)	.0	(. . .)
36	252	.000483	(80)	.000511	(29)	.0	(. . .)
37	253	.000990	(69)	.0	(. . .)	.000481	(69)
38	254	.001136	(64)	.000207	(51)	.0	(. . .)
39	261	.019459	(23)	.0	(. . .)	.018746	(25)
40	263	.007396	(41)	.000211	(50)	.011372	(36)
41	264	.012778	(31)	.0	(. . .)	.014621	(30)
42	265	.011289	(32)	.0	(. . .)	.013405	(34)
43	271	.016065	(27)	.0	(. . .)	.017918	(27)
44	272	.038857	(5)	.028182	(6)	.031187	(5)
45	273	.000220	(89)	.0	(. . .)	.006009	(52)
46	274	.019809	(21)	.000071	(61)	.019588	(20)
47	275	.030567	(11)	.0	(. . .)	.026473	(11)
48	278	.742537	(46)	.000452	(34)	.009682	(47)
49	281	.019411	(24)	.0	(. . .)	.019068	(19)
50	282	.000010	(99)	.000618	(20)	.007636	(50)
51	283	.030253	(13)	.000048	(64)	.025864	(12)
52	284	.017608	(25)	.0	(. . .)	.018238	(26)
53	285	.008560	(37)	.000842	(9)	.012903	(35)
54	286	.038352	(6)	.000998	(11)	.027835	(9)
55	287	.026124	(14)	.126193	(4)	.029372	(6)
56	291	.025163	(15)	.0	(. . .)	.023614	(14)
57	295	.000095	(96)	.000384	(37)	.000275	(78)
58	301	.048256	(4)	.210430	(2)	.035216	(4)
59	302	.006931	(42)	.0	(. . .)	.009180	(44)

	Industry Group	$\Delta = 5$ percent		$\Delta = 10$ percent		$\Delta = 15$ percent	
		% of Δ	Rank	% of Δ	Rank	% of Δ	Rank
60	307	.001449	(51)	.000670	(17)	.000396	(73)
61	311	.002959	(49)	.0	(...)	.009668	(42)
62	312	.001107	(67)	.0	(...)	.003062	(58)
63	314	.005889	(43)	.000031	(66)	.010096	(40)
64	321	.001190	(63)	.000032	(65)	.000329	(75)
65	322	.001375	(54)	.000679	(16)	.004669	(55)
66	324	.001214	(61)	.000483	(30)	.000328	(76)
67	325	.001021	(68)	.000169	(55)	.000006	(92)
68	326	.0	(...)	.000335	(43)	.003770	(57)
69	327	.001096	(75)	.0	(...)	.000542	(67)
70	328	.0	(...)	.0	(...)	.000035	(88)
71	331	.000178	(93)	.0	(...)	.0	(...)
72	332	.000017	(97)	.000355	(41)	.0	(...)
73	333	.0	(...)	.0	(...)	.0	(...)
74	335	.001329	(55)	.000548	(25)	.0	(...)
75	336	.0	(...)	.0	(...)	.0	(...)
76	339	.000259	(87)	.000521	(27)	.000097	(86)
77	341	.000919	(71)	.000121	(58)	.000786	(62)
78	342	.000010	(98)	.000667	(118)	.000381	(74)
79	343	.010755	(33)	.000464	(32)	.013982	(32)
80	344	.0	(...)	.0	(...)	.000559	(66)
81	345	.001283	(56)	.000171	(54)	.0	(...)
82	346	.000300	(86)	.000137	(57)	.000005	(93)
83	347	.000178	(92)	.000381	(38)	.000244	(81)
84	348	.000907	(72)	.0	(...)	.000019	(90)
85	349	.000399	(84)	.000781	(14)	.001153	(61)
86	351	.003063	(48)	.000305	(44)	.008324	(48)
87	352	.000932	(70)	.000725	(15)	.000021	(89)
88	353	.0	(...)	.0	(...)	.000270	(79)
89	354	.001212	(62)	.0	(...)	.008701	(46)
90	355	.000528	(79)	.0	(...)	.000053	(87)
91	356	.0	(...)	.0	(...)	.000423	(72)
92	357	.013124	(30)	.0	(...)	.013570	(33)
93	358	.001225	(60)	.000589	(24)	.004360	(56)
94	359	.001271	(57)	.000527	(26)	.0	(...)
95	361	.005352	(45)	.000298	(45)	.006709	(51)
96	362	.000203	(90)	.000518	(28)	.000561	(64)
97	363	.001461	(50)	.0	(...)	.0	(...)
98	364	.000680	(77)	.000794	(13)	.0	(...)
99	365	.001268	(58)	.000425	(36)	.0	(...)
100	366	.053216	(3)	.0	(...)	.037017	(3)
101	367	.001108	(66)	.000224	(49)	.0	(...)
102	369	.000122	(95)	.000089	(60)	.0	(...)
103	371	.000186	(91)	.000053	(63)	.000466	(71)
104	372	.008736	(36)	.000440	(35)	.011322	(38)
105	373	.000002	(100)	.000842	(8)	.000137	(82)
106	374	.0	(...)	.0	(...)	.0	(...)
107	375	.0	(...)	.0	(...)	.000480	(70)
108	381	.033812	(9)	.0	(...)	.023508	(15)
109	382	.000814	(73)	.000361	(40)	.0	(...)
110	383	.007740	(39)	.0	(...)	.009577	(43)
111	384	.019959	(20)	.0	(...)	.019477	(21)
112	386	.0	(...)	.000478	(31)	.0	(...)
113	387	.0	(...)	.0	(...)	.0	(...)
114	391	.005859	(44)	.0	(...)	.007915	(49)
115	393	.0	(...)	.0	(...)	.0	(...)
116	394	.000713	(76)	.000178	(53)	.000012	(91)
117	395	.000419	(83)	.000616	(21)	.002079	(60)
118	396	.000465	(81)	.0	(...)	.0	(...)

(continued)

Stockton

	Industry Group	Δ = 5 percent % of Δ	Rank	Δ = 10 percent % of Δ	Rank	Δ = 15 percent % of Δ	Rank
1	190	.000227	(67)	.000209	(60)	.000219	(39)
2	201	.001660	(9)	.000135	(68)	.000567	(17)
3	202	.001675	(8)	.000181	(62)	.000635	(6)
4	203	.0	(...)	.0	(...)	.0	(...)
5	204	.000109	(80)	.0	(...)	.0	(...)
6	205	.0	(...)	.000402	(46)	.0	(...)
7	206	.0	(...)	.000875	(12)	.0	(...)
8	207	.001109	(28)	.0	(...)	.0	(...)
9	028	.000115	(79)	.000275	(55)	.0	(...)
10	209	.000923	(36)	.0	(115)	.000490	(23)
11	211	.001232	(24)	.000298	(51)	.000031	(58)
12	212	.0	(...)	.000454	(43)	.0	(...)
13	221	.000744	(45)	.0	(...)	.000388	(29)
14	222	.001460	(19)	.0	(...)	.000310	(34)
15	223	.000711	(47)	.000174	(67)	.000578	(14)
16	224	.0	(...)	.0	(...)	.0	(...)
17	225	.000955	(34)	.000965	(6)	.000583	(12)
18	226	.000120	(78)	.0	(...)	.0	(...)
19	227	.000233	(66)	.000252	(57)	.0	(...)
20	228	.000196	(70)	.000890	(11)	.000211	(41)
21	229	.001231	(25)	.000802	(16)	.000581	(13)
22	231	.001648	(10)	.0	(...)	.0	(...)
23	232	.000187	(72)	.0	(...)	.000566	(16)
24	233	.001628	(12)	.000670	(32)	.0	(...)
25	234	.001559	(16)	.000585	(35)	.000030	(59)
26	235	.0	(...)	.000685	(30)	.0	(...)
27	236	.0	(...)	.0	(...)	.0	(...)
28	237	.000312	(62)	.0	(...)	.000473	(24)
29	239	.001430	(20)	.000501	(40)	.0	(...)
30	241	.001159	(26)	.0	(...)	.0	(...)
31	242	.000051	(81)	.000284	(53)	.000190	(44)
32	243	.0	(...)	.0	(...)	.000544	(19)
33	244	.0	(...)	.000798	(18)	.0	(...)
34	249	.001099	(29)	.000773	(22)	.000422	(26)
35	251	.001576	(15)	.000096	(71)	.0	(...)
36	252	.000788	(43)	.000698	(28)	.000623	(8)
37	253	.000309	(63)	.000175	(64)	.000111	(50)
38	254	.0	(...)	.0	(...)	.000058	(55)
39	261	.000172	(73)	.000294	(52)	.000415	(27)
40	263	.000571	(53)	.000207	(61)	.000533	(20)
41	264	.000817	(41)	.000091	(72)	.0	(...)
42	265	.0	(...)	.0	(...)	.0	(...)
43	271	.0	(...)	.000559	(37)	.000595	(11)
44	272	.0	(...)	.000969	(5)	.0	(...)
45	273	.0	(...)	.000097	(70)	.0002	(36)
46	274	.000817	(40)	.000949	(88)	.000289	(35)
47	275	.000153	(75)	.000223	(59)	.0	(...)
48	278	.000193	(71)	.000413	(45)	.000164	(46)
49	281	.000163	(74)	.000869	(14)	.0	(...)
50	282	.000663	(49)	.0	(...)	.0	(...)
51	283	.000551	(54)	.000719	(27)	.000083	(53)
52	284	.000045	(82)	.000466	(42)	.0	(...)
53	285	.000344	(60)	.000657	(33)	.0	(89)
54	286	.000999	(32)	.000327	(49)	.000110	(51)
55	287	.831648	(1)	.681614	(1)	.667876	(1)
56	291	.0	(...)	.0	(...)	.000572	(15)
57	295	.001692	(6)	.0	(...)	.0	(...)
58	301	.000816	(42)	.0	(...)	.000369	(32)
59	302	.000244	(65)	.000439	(44)	.000633	(7)

	Industry Group	Δ = 5 percent		Δ = 10 percent		Δ = 15 percent	
		% of Δ	Rank	% of Δ	Rank	% of Δ	Rank
60	307	.0	(...)	.0	(...)	.0	(...)
61	311	.001144	(27)	.000725	(25)	.0	(...)
62	312	.001856	(3)	.000926	(9)	.000315	(33)
63	314	.000148	(76)	.000798	(19)	.000556	(18)
64	321	.000777	(44)	.000971	(4)	.000618	(9)
65	322	.000615	(51)	.000800	(17)	.000113	(48)
66	324	.001740	(5)	.0	(...)	.0	(...)
67	325	.0	(...)	.000239	(58)	.000148	(47)
68	326	.000910	(37)	.000686	(29)	.0	(...)
69	327	.000394	(59)	.000519	(39)	.000644	(5)
70	328	.001635	(11)	.000618	(34)	.000004	(61)
71	331	.175892	(2)	.212871	(2)	.210029	(2)
72	332	.0	(...)	.0	(...)	.0	(...)
73	333	.001375	(22)	.0	(...)	.0	(...)
74	335	.0	(...)	.0	(...)	.0	(...)
75	336	.000661	(50)	.000356	(48)	.0	(...)
76	339	.0	(...)	.0	(...)	.0	(...)
77	341	.001403	(21)	.000535	(38)	.0	(...)
78	342	.0	(...)	.0	(...)	.0	(...)
79	343	.000135	(77)	.000301	(50)	.000650	(4)
80	344	.000035	(83)	.000682	(31)	.0	(...)
81	345	.000428	(56)	.000177	(63)	.000510	(21)
82	346	.0	(...)	.0	(...)	.000373	(31)
83	347	.001368	(23)	.0	(...)	.0	(...)
84	348	.001765	(4)	.000829	(15)	.000001	(62)
85	349	.0	(...)	.0	(...)	.0	(...)
86	351	.0	(...)	.000175	(65)	.000567	(16)
87	352	.0	(...)	.0	(...)	.0	(...)
88	353	.000665	(48)	.000794	(21)	.0	(...)
89	354	.0	(...)	.0	(...)	.0	(...)
90	355	.000205	(68)	.0	(...)	.0	(...)
91	356	.000545	(55)	.000951	(7)	.000044	(56)
92	357	.001524	(17)	.000739	(24)	.0	(...)
93	358	.000199	(69)	.0	(...)	.0	(...)
94	359	.001605	(14)	.000262	(56)	.000266	(73)
95	361	.0	(...)	.000868	(113)	.0	(...)
96	362	.0	(...)	.0	(...)	.000222	(38)
97	363	.001611	(13)	.0	(...)	.0	(...)
98	364	.000712	(46)	.000797	(20)	.0	(...)
99	365	.0	(...)	.0	(...)	.0	(...)
100	366	.000976	(33)	.000890	(110)	.000090	(52)
101	367	.0	(...)	.0	(...)	.0	(...)
102	369	.001005	(31)	.000724	(26)	.000461	(25)
103	371	.0	(...)	.107365	(3)	.128363	(3)
104	372	.000884	(38)	.00574	(36)	.000500	(22)
105	373	.0	(...)	.0	(...)	.0	(...)
106	374	.0	(...)	.000174	(66)	.000201	(43)
107	375	.001040	(30)	.0	(...)	.0	(...)
108	381	.001689	(7)	.000382	(47)	.000407	(28)
109	382	.000398	(58)	.000745	(23)	.000211	(40)
110	383	.000513	(57)	.0	(...)	.000213	(42)
111	384	.000325	(61)	.0	(...)	.000069	(54)
112	386	.0	(...)	.0	(...)	.000608	(10)
113	387	.000609	(64)	.000112	(69)	.0	(...)
114	391	.000950	(35)	.000494	(41)	.000042	(57)
115	393	.000576	(52)	.0	(...)	.000174	(45)
116	394	.0	(...)	.0	(...)	.0	(...)
117	395	.000862	(39)	.0	(...)	.000388	(30)
118	396	.001521	(18)	.000282	(54)	.000111	(49)

Source: Calculated by the author.

1. Arrow, Kenneth. Essays in the Theory of Risk Bearing. Chicago: Markham, 1971.

2. Bahl, Roy W.; Firestine, Robert; and Phares, Donald. "Industrial Diversity in Urban Areas: Alternative Measures and Inter-metropolitan Comparisons." Economic Geography 47 (July 1971): 414-25.

3. Borts, George H. "Regional Cycles of Manufacturing Employment in the U.S., 1914-53." National Bureau of Economic Research, Occasional Paper No. 75, 1961.

4. Clark, J. M. Strategic Factors in Business Cycles. New York: Harper and Row, 1934.

5. Conroy, Michael E. "Alternative Strategies for Regional Industrial Diversification." Journal of Regional Science 14 (April 1974): 1, 36-51.

6. ____. "The Concept and Measurement of Regional Industrial Diversification." Southern Economic Journal January 1975.

7. ____. "The Optimal Diversification of Regional Industrial Structures." Regional and Urban Economics Forthcoming.

8. ____. "Optimal Regional Industrial Diversification: A Portfolio-Analytic Approach." Ph.D. Dissertation, University of Illinois at Urbana-Champaign, 1972.

9. Cootner, P. H. The Random Character of Stock Market Prices. Cambridge, Mass.: National Bureau of Economic Research, 1964.

10. Cutler, Addison T., and Hansz, James E. "Sensitivity of Cities to Economic Fluctuations." Growth and Change 2 (January 1971): 23-28.

11. Engerman, S. "Regional Aspects of Stabilization Policy." Essays in Fiscal Federalism. Edited by R. A. Musgrace. Washington, D.C.: The Brookings Institution, 1965.

12. Feldstein, M. S. "Mean-Variance Analysis in the Theory of Liquidity Preference and Portfolio Selection." Review of Economic Studies 26 (January 1969): 13-14.

13. Florence, P. Sargent. Investment, Location and Size of Plant. Cambridge: Oxford University Press, 1948.

14. Garbarino, J. W. "Some Implications of Regional and Industrial Differences in Unemployment." Proceedings of the Twenty-Ninth Annual Conference of the Western Economics Association. Portland, Ore., 1954, pp. 28-32.

15. Goldberger, Arthur S. Topics in Regression Analysis. New York: John Wiley, 1968.

16. Goldfarb, Donald, "GRADMAX, A Variable Metric Algorithm for Solving Nonlinear Programming Problems with Linear Constraints." Mimeo, 1971.

17. Gomory, R. E. "An Algorithm for the Mixed Integer Problem." Santa Monica, Calif: The Rand Corporation, RM2597, 1960.

18. Hador, Josef, and Russell, William R. "Stochastic Dominance and Diversification." Journal of Economic Theory 3 (1971): 288-305.

19. Hanna, Frank A. "Cyclical and Secular Changes in State Per Capita Incomes, 1929-50." Review of Economics and Statistics 36 (August 1954): 320-30.

20. Hanoch, G., and Levy, H. "Efficiency Analysis of Choices Involving Risk." Review of Economic Studies 36 (July 1969): 335-46.

21. Hicks, J. F. "Liquidity." Economic Journal 72 (1962): 787-802.

22. Industrial Development Research Institute. Site Selection Handbook, 1971. Vol. 2. Atlanta: Conway Research Corporation, 1971.

23. Isard, Walter. Methods of Regional Analysis. Cambridge, Mass: MIT Press, 1960.

24. Kidner, Frank L. California Business Cycles. Los Angeles: UCLA Press, 1946.

25. Land, A. H., and Doig, A. "An Automatic Method of Solving Discrete Programming Problems." Econometrica 28 (1960): 497-520.

26. Latham, William R., III. "The Impact of Agglomerative Economies on Industrial Location." Ph. D. dissertation, University of Illinois, 1973.

27. Leven, Charles. "Establishing Goals for Regional Economic Development." Regional Development and Planning. Edited by John Friedmann and William Alonso. Cambridge, Mass.: MIT Press, 1964.

28. Lintner, John. "Valuation of Risk Assets." Review of Economics and Statistics 79 (February 1965): 13-37.

29. ____. "Optimum Dividends and Uncertainty." Quarterly Journal of Economics 18 (February 1964): 49-95.

30. Lovell, Michael C. "Seasonal Adjustment of Economic Time Series and Multiple Regression Analysis." Journal of the American Statistical Association 37 (December 1963): 993-1010.

31. Madansky, A. "Methods of Solution of Linear Programs Under Uncertainty." Operations Research 10 (July-August 1962): 463-71.

32. Markowitz, Harry M. "Portfolio Selection." Journal of Finance 7 (March 1952): 77-91.

33. ____. Portfolio Selection, Efficient Diversification of Investments. Chicago: Cowles Foundation for Economic Analysis, 1959.

34. McLaughlin, Glenn. "Industrial Diversification in American Cities." Quarterly Journal of Economics 44 (November 1930): 131-49.

35. McMillan, Claude, Jr. Mathematical Programming. New York: John Wiley, 1971.

36. Neff, Phillip. "Interregional Cyclical Differentials: Causes, Measurement, and Significance." Papers and Proceedings of the American Economic Association 39 (May 1949): 105-19.

37. ____, and Weifenbach, Annette. Business Cycles in Selected Industrial Areas. Berkeley: University of California Press, 1949.

38. Nerlove, Marc, "Spectral Analysis of Seasonal Adjustment Procedures." Econometrica 32 (July 1964): 241-86.

39. Nie, Norman H.; Bert, Dale H.; and Hull, C. Hadlai. SPSS, Statistical Package for the Social Sciences. New York: McGraw-Hill, 1970.

40. Nourse, Hugh O. Regional Economics. New York: McGraw-Hill, 1968.

41. Pratt, John W. "Risk Aversion in the Small and in the Large." Econometrica 32 (January-April 1964): 122-36.

42. Reinwald, L. T. "Some Aspects of Statistically Interpreting the Manufacturing Functions of United States Cities." M.A. thesis, Clark University, 1949.

43. Richardson, Harry W. Regional Economics. New York: Praeger, 1969.

44. Richter, Charles. "Cardinal Utility, Portfolio Selection, and Taxation." Review of Economic Studies 25 (1957): 49-52.

45. Rodgers, A. "Some Aspects of Industrial Diversification in the United States." Economic Geography 33 (January 1957): 16-30.

46. Rothschild, Michael and Stiglitz, Joseph E. "Increasing Risk I: A Definition." Journal of Economic Theory 2 (1970): 225-43.

47. ____. "Increasing Risk II: Its Economic Consequences." Journal of Economic Theory 3 (1971): 66-84.

48. Roy, A. D. "Safety First and the Holding of Assets." Econometrica 20 (July 1952): 431-49.

49. Samuelson, Paul A. "The Fundamental Approximation Theorem of Portfolio Analysis in Terms of Means, Variances and Higher Moments." Review of Economic Studies 37 (October 1970): 537-42.

50. ____. "General Proof that Diversification Pays." Journal of Financial and Quantitative Analysis 2 (March 1967): 1-13.

51. Sharpe, William F. Portfolio Theory and Capital Markets. New York: McGraw-Hill, 1970.

52. ____. "A Simplified Model for Portfolio Analysis." Management Science (January 1963): 277-93.

53. Siegel, Richard A. "Do Regional Business Cycles Exist?" Western Economic Journal 5 (December 1966); 44-57.

54. Simpson, Paul P. Regional Aspects of Business Cycles and Special Studies of the Pacific Northwest. Eugene, Ore.: Bonneville Adminstration and the University of Oregon, 1953.

55. Steigenga, W. "A Comparative Analysis and Classification of Netherlands Towns." Tijdschrift voor Economische en Sociale Geografie (June-July 1955): pp. 105-18.

56. Takayama, T., and Judge, George. Spatial and Temporal Allocation Models. Amsterdam: North-Holland, 1971.

57. Thompson, Wilbur. A Preface to Urban Economics. Baltimore: Johns Hopkins University Press, 1956.

58. ____. "The Economic Base of Urban Problems." Contemporary Economic Issues. Edited by Neil W. Chamberlain. Homewood, Ill.: Richard D. Irwin, 1969.

59. Tobin, James. "Comment on Borch and Feldstein." Review of Economic Studies 36 (January 1969): 13-14.

60. ____. "Liquidity Preference as Behavior Towards Risk." Review of Economic Studies 25 (February 1958): 65-85.

61. Tress, R. C. "Unemployment and Diversification of Industry." The Manchester School 9 (1938): 140-52.

62. Tsiang, S. C. "The Rationale of the Mean-Standard Deviation Analysis, Skewness Preference, and the Demand for Money." Department of Economics Discussion Paper No. 2, Cornell University, April 1971.

63. Ullman, E. L., and Dacey, Michael F. The Economic Base of American Cities. Seattle: University of Washington Press, 1969.

64. ____. "The Minimum Requirements Approach to the Urban Economic Base." Papers and Proceedings of the Regional Science Association 6 (1960): 175-94.

65. U.S., Department of Commerce, Bureau of the Census. County and City Data Book, 1967. Washington, D. C.: Government Printing Office, 1966.

66. ____. "The Location of Manufacturing Plants by County, Industry, and Employment Size." 1963 Census of Manufactures, Special Reports. Washington, D. C.: Government Printing Office, 1966.

67. U.S., Department of Labor, Bureau of Labor Statistics. Employment and Earnings. Vol. 4-14. Washington, D. C.: Government Printing Office, 1958-67.

68. _____. Employment and Earnings, United States, 1909-68. Washington, D. C.: Government Printing Office, 1970.

69. U.S., Executive Office of the President, Office of Statistical Standards. Standard Industrial Classification Manual, 1957. Washington, D. C.: Government Printing Office, 1957.

70. _____. Standard Industrial Classification Manual, 1967. Washington, D. C.: Government Printing Office, 1967.

71. _____. Standard Industrial Classification Manual, Supplement to 1957 Edition, 1963. Washington, D. C.: Government Printing Office, 1963.

72. _____. Standard Metropolitan Statistical Areas, 1967. Washington, D. C.: Government Printing Office, 1967.

73. Vining, Rutledge. "Location of Industry and Regional Patterns of Business-Cycle Behavior." Econometrica 14 (January 1961): 37-68.

74. _____. "Regional Variation in Cyclical Fluctuations Viewed as a Frequency Distribution." Econometrica 13 (July 1945): 183-213.

75. _____. "The Region as a Concept in Business-Cycle Analysis." Econometrica 14 (July 1946): 201-18.

76. _____. "The Region as an Economic Entity and Certain Variations to be Observed in the Study of Systems of Regions." Papers and Proceedings of the American Economic Association 39 (May 1949): 89-104.

77. Williams, Robert M. "The Timing and Amplitude of Regional Business Cycles." Papers and Proceedings of the Pacific Coast Economics Association 4 (1950): 47-51.

78. Wonnacott, Ronald J., and Wonnacott, Thomas H. Econometrics. New York: John Wiley, 1970.

of manufacturing employment,
the, 47; lognormal distribution,
116; skewness, 17; spread of,
17; stochastic nature, 17, 18;
variations over time, 16
Richardson, Harry W., 2, 92, 105
Richter, Charles, 116
risk, 43, 115; financial returns, 15;
instability in returns, 15
risk-averse policy makers, 24
risk aversion, 27, 85; decreasing
absolute, 116; decreasing or
constant absolute, 115; individual, of the,85
risk indifference curve, 28
risk indifference function, 27
risk-compensated expected income,
86
risk-compensated real income, 87
risk-premium income, 85
risk-return transformation curve, 26
Rodgers, A., 9
Rothschild, Michael, 117
Roy, A. D., 117

sample of regions, 48, 50
Samuelson, Paul A., 23, 118
seasonal variation, as an object of
stabilization policy , 54
semivariance, 116
sensitivity index, 5
sensitivity of a region to fluctuations
in the national economy, 8;
industrial composition, 8; separation theorem, 25, 40
Sharpe, William F., 23, 26, 115
Siegel, Richard A., 1, 2, 7, 54
Simpson, Paul P., 1
simulation of industry increments, 93
spatial equilibrium, 84, 112; labor
force, of the 85, 113; net revenue maximizing formulation, 35-
36; under uncertainty, 88
spatial programming, 33; basic linear,
33; determinate, 16; regional
and interregional, 33; simple
stochastic extension, 34;

stochastic, 16
specialization, 28; advantages,
2, 29; amplitude of fluc-
tuation, 4; complete, 23;
durable goods, 3; gains
from, 29; in durable goods
manufacturing, 8; manu-
facturing, in, 4
stabilization policy, 1
Standard Industrial Classifications, 12; groupings,
14; revisions of the code,
49
Steigenga, W., 9
Stiglitz, Jos. E. (see Michael
Rothschild)
stochastic dominance, 116, 117
Stockton, California, 98
subsidy, diversifying industries,
91

Takayama, T., 33, 35, 37
technologies, alternative, 16
theoretical stability, 45
Thompson, Wilbur, 1, 2, 13,
54, 77, 92, 105
Tobin, James, 116, 118
treatment of seasonality, 54
Tress, R. C., 9
Tsiang, S. C., 115, 118

Ullman, E. L., 10
uncertainty, in the labor
market, 85; in returns, 15,
85
unemployment compensation, 86
unemployment rate, 109
usable SMSA, 48
utility function, 27, 115;
investor's, 116; quadratic,
116
utility maximizing investor, 115
utility theory, 16; recent criticism, 115

variance, 17; appropriate measure
of the fluctuations in returns,

as the, 44; appropriate measure
of risk, as an, 96; measure of
relative riskiness, as a, 116;
specific measure of the "riskiness" of a stochastic process,
as a, 115
variance-covariance matrix, 106; as
relative covariances, 63; estimated, 48-49; for employment,
47
Vining, Rutledge, 1, 3, 5

Weifenbach, Annette (see Phillip Neff)
Williams, Robert M., 1, 4
Wonnacott, Ronald J., and Wonna-
cott, Thomas H., 55

ABOUT THE AUTHOR

MICHAEL E. CONROY is Assistant Professor of Economics at the University of Texas at Austin.

A recent graduate of the University of Illinois at Urbana-Champaign, Dr. Conroy has published in the area of urban and regional development in the Journal of Regional Science, Southern Economic Journal, Land Economics, and Growth and Change.

Dr. Conroy holds a B.A. from Tulane University and an M.S. and a Ph.D. from the University of Illinois.

INDUSTRIAL DIVERSIFICATION IN ZAMBIA
Alistair Young

INDUSTRIAL LOCATION IN METROPOLITAN AREAS: A General Model
Tested for Boston
Donald N. Stone

REGIONAL ECONOMIC ANALYSIS FOR PRACTITIONERS: An Introduction
to Common Descriptive Methods
Avrom Bendavid